HOMOSEXUALITY

Opposing Viewpoints®

Other Books of Related Interest

HOMOSEXUALITY

Opposing Viewpoints®

Auriana Ojeda, *Book Editor*

Daniel Leone, *President*
Bonnie Szumski, *Publisher*
Scott Barbour, *Managing Editor*
Helen Cothran, *Senior Editor*

OPPOSING
VIEWPOINTS®
SERIES

GREENHAVEN
PRESS®

THOMSON
™
GALE

San Diego • Detroit • New York • San Francisco • Cleveland
New Haven, Conn. • Waterville, Maine • London • Munich

THOMSON

✶ ™

GALE

© 2004 by Greenhaven Press. Greenhaven Press is an imprint of The Gale Group, Inc., a division of Thomson Learning, Inc.

Greenhaven® and Thomson Learning™ are trademarks used herein under license.

For more information, contact
Greenhaven Press
27500 Drake Rd.
Farmington Hills, MI 48331-3535
Or you can visit our Internet site at http://www.gale.com

Cover credit: © Creatas

LIBRARY OF CONGRESS CATALOGING-IN-PUBLICATION DATA

Homosexuality / Auriana Ojeda, book editor.
    p. cm. — (Opposing viewpoints series)
    Includes bibliographical references and index.
    ISBN 0-7377-1688-6 (pbk. : alk. paper) — ISBN 0-7377-1687-8 (lib. : alk. paper)
      1. Homosexuality—United States. 2. Gender identity—United States.
    3. Homophobia—United States. 4. Homosexuality—Moral and ethical aspects—
    United States. 5. Gay rights—United States. I. Ojeda, Auriana, 1977– .
    II. Opposing viewpoints series (Unnumbered)
    HQ76.3.U5 H6443 2004
    306.76'6'0973—dc21   2003044859

Printed in the United States of America

"Congress shall make no law. . . abridging the freedom of speech, or of the press."

First Amendment to the U.S. Constitution

The basic foundation of our democracy is the First Amendment guarantee of freedom of expression. The Opposing Viewpoints Series is dedicated to the concept of this basic freedom and the idea that it is more important to practice it than to enshrine it.

Contents

Why Consider Opposing Viewpoints?

"The only way in which a human being can make some approach to knowing the whole of a subject is by hearing what can be said about it by persons of every variety of opinion and studying all modes in which it can be looked at by every character of mind. No wise man ever acquired his wisdom in any mode but this."

John Stuart Mill

In our media-intensive culture it is not difficult to find differing opinions. Thousands of newspapers and magazines and dozens of radio and television talk shows resound with differing points of view. The difficulty lies in deciding which opinion to agree with and which "experts" seem the most credible. The more inundated we become with differing opinions and claims, the more essential it is to hone critical reading and thinking skills to evaluate these ideas. Opposing Viewpoints books address this problem directly by presenting stimulating debates that can be used to enhance and teach these skills. The varied opinions contained in each book examine many different aspects of a single issue. While examining these conveniently edited opposing views, readers can develop critical thinking skills such as the ability to compare and contrast authors' credibility, facts, argumentation styles, use of persuasive techniques, and other stylistic tools. In short, the Opposing Viewpoints Series is an ideal way to attain the higher-level thinking and reading skills so essential in a culture of diverse and contradictory opinions.

In addition to providing a tool for critical thinking, Opposing Viewpoints books challenge readers to question their own strongly held opinions and assumptions. Most people form their opinions on the basis of upbringing, peer pressure, and personal, cultural, or professional bias. By reading carefully balanced opposing views, readers must directly confront new ideas as well as the opinions of those with whom they disagree. This is not to simplistically argue that everyone who reads opposing views will—or should—change his or her opinion. Instead, the series enhances readers' understanding of their own views by encouraging confrontation with opposing ideas. Careful examination of others' views can lead to the readers' understanding of the logical inconsistencies in their own opinions, perspective on why they hold an opinion, and the consideration of the possibility that their opinion requires further evaluation.

Evaluating Other Opinions

To ensure that this type of examination occurs, Opposing Viewpoints books present all types of opinions. Prominent spokespeople on different sides of each issue as well as well-known professionals from many disciplines challenge the reader. An additional goal of the series is to provide a forum for other, less known, or even unpopular viewpoints. The opinion of an ordinary person who has had to make the decision to cut off life support from a terminally ill relative, for example, may be just as valuable and provide just as much insight as a medical ethicist's professional opinion. The editors have two additional purposes in including these less known views. One, the editors encourage readers to respect others' opinions—even when not enhanced by professional credibility. It is only by reading or listening to and objectively evaluating others' ideas that one can determine whether they are worthy of consideration. Two, the inclusion of such viewpoints encourages the important critical thinking skill of objectively evaluating an author's credentials and bias. This evaluation will illuminate an author's reasons for taking a particular stance on an issue and will aid in readers' evaluation of the author's ideas.

It is our hope that these books will give readers a deeper understanding of the issues debated and an appreciation of the complexity of even seemingly simple issues when good and honest people disagree. This awareness is particularly important in a democratic society such as ours in which people enter into public debate to determine the common good. Those with whom one disagrees should not be regarded as enemies but rather as people whose views deserve careful examination and may shed light on one's own.

Thomas Jefferson once said that "difference of opinion leads to inquiry, and inquiry to truth." Jefferson, a broadly educated man, argued that "if a nation expects to be ignorant and free . . . it expects what never was and never will be." As individuals and as a nation, it is imperative that we consider the opinions of others and examine them with skill and discernment. The Opposing Viewpoints Series is intended to help readers achieve this goal.

David L. Bender and Bruno Leone,
Founders

Greenhaven Press anthologies primarily consist of previously published material taken from a variety of sources, including periodicals, books, scholarly journals, newspapers, government documents, and position papers from private and public organizations. These original sources are often edited for length and to ensure their accessibility for a young adult audience. The anthology editors also change the original titles of these works in order to clearly present the main thesis of each viewpoint and to explicitly indicate the opinion presented in the viewpoint. These alterations are made in consideration of both the reading and comprehension levels of a young adult audience. Every effort is made to ensure that Greenhaven Press accurately reflects the original intent of the authors included in this anthology.

Introduction

"[Homosexuals] have moved from being a social movement to more of an interest group with established lobbying groups, political-action committees and a distinctive voting profile. It's a group that is out and is exercising influence."

—*Steve Sanders*, Insight on the News,
November 27, 2000

On June 27, 1969, police raided a gay bar in New York City called the Stonewall Inn to enforce vice laws against homosexual behavior. Such raids, in which police often harassed homosexuals, were common in the 1950s and 1960s. In this instance, however, the patrons of the bar rebelled against the police, and members of the surrounding community, most of whom were also gay, joined the revolt. The ensuing riot, which became known as the Stonewall Rebellion, lasted for three days and spawned a newly unified and empowered homosexual community. According to author Roger E. Biery, the event brought visibility and togetherness to many gays and lesbians who had previously felt isolated: "For the first time in history, it was okay to be gay." The Stonewall riots exemplify the tension that has always existed between homosexuals and the rest of society.

Inspired by Stonewall and the civil rights and antiwar movements of the 1960s, gays and lesbians increased their efforts to announce their existence and improve social acceptance of homosexuality. Their first goal was to encourage people to "come out of the closet," that is, publicly proclaim their homosexuality. Thousands of people did just that, and they engendered a social change movement that has grown substantially. The number of gay and lesbian organizations grew from around fifty in 1969 to almost eight hundred in 1973 and several thousand by 1990. In 1970 five thousand gays and lesbians marched in New York City to commemorate the first anniversary of the Stonewall riots. In 1987 over six hundred thousand gays and lesbians marched in Washington, D.C., to demand equality and civil rights. Since then, thousands of "gay pride" parades and events have taken place every year.

In the three decades following the Stonewall Rebellion, the gay rights movement won significant advances in social acceptance. By 1990 half of the states had decriminalized homosexual behavior, and police harassment of homosexual establishments was reduced. Wisconsin and Massachusetts were the first states to include sexual orientation in their civil rights statutes, and many other states followed their lead. In 1975 the Civil Service Commission eliminated the ban on the employment of homosexuals in most federal jobs. In 1974, the American Psychiatric Association removed homosexuality from the *Diagnostic and Statistical Manual of Mental Disorders*, and in 1981, the World Health Organization removed homosexuality from its list of illnesses. Denmark became the first country to recognize same-sex couples in 1989. Finally, in 2000, Vermont became the first state to offer same-sex couples most of the rights and privileges of marriage under new arrangements called "civil unions."

The gay liberation movement faced significant obstacles in its crusade for greater visibility and social acceptance for homosexuals. One of the most damaging setbacks was the AIDS crisis, which surfaced in the 1980s. Doctors first recognized AIDS in 1981, but HIV, the virus that causes AIDS, was not isolated until 1983. Hundreds of thousands of gay men died from AIDS throughout the 1980s and early 1990s. Experts estimate that during the mid-1980s, nearly one hundred thousand new HIV infections surfaced each year. Newspaper headlines announced the dawn of a "gay plague," and the progress toward gay civil rights was interrupted. As stated by author Edmund White, "When AIDS was first identified, it was called gay cancer, and gays feared massive quarantines, even internment in concentration camps. To be sure, many gays have lost jobs, apartments and friends because they had the disease or were suspected of having it."

Devastated by the epidemic, gay and lesbian activists focused their efforts on expanding funding for AIDS research and on developing AIDS awareness campaigns. They created a host of organizations, such as the Gay Men's Health

Crisis in New York City, to provide services and assistance to those infected. Local and national organizations also grew in size and number as the community joined together in the fight against AIDS. Activists developed education programs that stressed condom use as the most effective protection against contracting the disease. According to free-lance journalist Anne Christiansen Bullers, "The campaigns were often controversial, but AIDS researchers believe that they were effective, and helped to slow the spread of the disease both within at-risk communities and outside them." The activists' efforts were indeed rewarded; the number of new AIDS cases in the United States dropped from 60,805 in 1996 to 41,311 in 2001.

In addition to fighting the AIDS epidemic, the gay liberation movement has battled opposition from conservative and religious circles. One of the most notorious protestors, singer Anita Bryant, launched a successful campaign to repeal a gay rights ordinance in Dade County, Florida, in 1977. Her success encouraged others, and by the early 1980s, a strong conservative backlash against the gay rights movement had formed. Some states repealed gay civil rights ordinances and some reinstated laws against homosexual acts. In 1982 the U.S. Department of Defense issued a policy stating that homosexuality is incompatible with military service. In 1986 President Ronald Reagan cut funding for AIDS research, and Pope John Paul II called homosexuals "intrinsically disordered" and "evil." Efforts to stifle the gay rights movement, coupled with significant losses to the AIDS virus, cost gays and lesbians much of their hard-won progress.

Over the last ten years, the gay rights movement has regained much of the public support that it lost in the 1980s, but true equality between homosexuals and heterosexuals has yet to be realized. The 1990s debate over whether gays and lesbians have the right to marry epitomizes the decades-old battle between homosexual supporters and antigay activists. Many gays and lesbians contend that each person has a fundamental right to choose whom he or she wishes to marry; what gender that person is should be irrelevant. Antigay advocates argue that marriage is, and always should be, defined as the union of one man and one woman. Conservatives struck a blow to the gay rights movement in 1996 with the passage of the Defense of Marriage Act, which denies federal recognition of same-sex marriages and gives states the right to refuse to recognize same-sex marriages licensed in other states. Gays and lesbians celebrated their own victory in 2000 when Vermont created civil unions as a way to enable gay and lesbian couples to enjoy many of the same legal rights enjoyed by married couples. Many gays and lesbians consider civil unions a positive step toward equal rights for homosexuals but believe that full equality will only be achieved when same-sex couples have access to conventional marriage.

The conflict over marriage rights for homosexuals illustrates the ambivalence with which society has viewed the gay rights movement since Stonewall. Increased visibility brought significant social changes and enabled gays and lesbians to live and love more openly than they ever had before. Greater visibility also brought vehement protests and denunciations of homosexuals. *Homosexuality: Opposing Viewpoints* examines the gay liberation movement and other issues in the following chapters: What Are the Origins of Homosexuality? Should Society Encourage Increased Acceptance of Homosexuality? Is Homosexuality Immoral? Should Society Sanction Gay and Lesbian Families? The viewpoints presented in this volume demonstrate that homosexuality remains a controversial issue in American society and politics.

CHAPTER 1

What Are the Origins of Homosexuality?

Chapter Preface

The question of why some people are attracted to members of their own sex has led to a wide range of answers throughout history. In their attempt to identify the origins of homosexuality, biologists, sociologists, religious leaders, psychologists, and psychiatrists have proposed theories that many people consider absurd. For example, in the eighteenth and nineteenth centuries, medical textbooks claimed that homosexuality was a sign of moral depravity and was caused by demonic possession. Controversial theories explaining the origins of homosexuality have not been consigned to the history books, however. One recent theory, advocated by medical doctors William Wong and Doris Rapp, posits that male babies raised on soy-based formula, instead of milk-based formula or breast milk, may grow up to be gay.

Soy contains compounds called isoflavones (also known as phytoestrogens) that mimic estrogen, the primary female hormone that induces puberty and regulates a woman's reproductive system. According to Wong, Rapp, and others, isoflavones cause numerous health problems in children, including poor growth and brain development, vitamin deficiencies, kidney problems, and sterility. In addition, they argue, isoflavones interfere with the surge of testosterone that male infants undergo in their first few months of life, a hormonal influx that programs them to develop male characteristics when they hit puberty. When male babies ingest soy-based formula, these doctors contend, the flood of female hormones may delay the onset of puberty, which typically begins around the age of thirteen. Delayed puberty, in the doctors' opinions, can affect a boy's sexual orientation. As stated by Wong, "Male children fed soy formulas and soy products may not ever get to like girls."

Naturopathic doctor and ordained minister Stephen Byrnes disagrees with Wong and Rapp, stating that "when it comes to the claim that isoflavones are responsible for causing homosexuality, there is neither science nor common sense at work." According to Byrnes, Wong and Rapp suggest that hormones, particularly estrogen, determine sexual orientation. By this rationale, Byrnes argues, men who have sex with men are acting like women, because they are driven by female hormones. But Byrnes maintains that certain ancient cultures, such as the Celts and the Greeks, indulged in and glorified male homosexual behavior. These societies, and many others, denigrated women and viewed them as inferior beings. As stated by Colin Spencer in *Homosexuality in History*, the purpose of homosexual behavior in these and other cultures was to induce "maleness" and "male loving was loosely entwined with valor, heroism, bravery and manliness." Thus, Byrnes argues, in some societies, homosexual behavior was not viewed as effeminate, as Wong and Rapp suggest, but as evidence of a man's masculinity. Byrnes concludes that "the idea that isoflavones have an effect on human sexual behavior is a bad one that needs to be cut off at the knees."

The theory that isoflavones cause homosexuality is one of many explanations for homosexuality that most experts, like Byrnes, consider illogical. Most sexuality professionals today agree that homosexuality results from a combination of biological and cultural factors. However, researchers still do not know exactly what drives some people to be attracted to members of the same sex. The authors in the following chapter examine many of the most recent theories about the origins of homosexuality. These theories are important because much is at stake in exploring why some people become gay. For gay activists, exploring the factors that contribute to homosexuality may make the concept less exotic to the heterosexual community and thus create a more tolerant society for people of all sexual orientations. On the other hand, many conservatives hope that research will show once and for all that homosexuality is not biological in origin but is instead pathological and immoral.

"Sexual orientation . . . is . . . genetically and biologically innate and determined."

Homosexuality Is Biologically Determined

Warren C. Lathe III

The following viewpoint is excerpted from a speech given by Warren C. Lathe III, a molecular biologist, to a congregation of the Church of Jesus Christ and Latter-Day Saints in Salt Lake City, Utah. Lathe argues that biology determines sexual orientation. He contends that some scientists have found differences in the brain anatomies between heterosexual and homosexual men while others have discovered that chromosomes seem to have a role in determining sexual orientation. Acknowledging that homosexuality has a biological component, Lathe argues, is important for promoting tolerance and acceptance of gays and lesbians.

As you read, consider the following questions:

1. According to the author, how can forgoing reproduction in favor of an organism's kin be advantageous?
2. What are the two reasons Lathe gives for why traits seen in animals might also be seen in humans?
3. As quoted by the author, where in the body does Dean Hamer find the origin of homosexuality?

[In 1996] LDS Social Services[1] put out a pamphlet that puts forth a very simple explanation for a very complex human behavior. It puts forth a dichotomy that is false. It puts forth a dichotomy that is an "either" or an "or" proposition. And, it puts forth a treatment plan that is based upon this simple and false dichotomy.

Cause for Concern

I have come here today because I am concerned for three reasons: First: I am a believing convert to the Mormon church and unrepentant in that. Second: I am a gay male who has gone through LDS Social Services therapy and knows the destructive and debilitating effect it can have on a man's spirituality. And, third: I am a molecular biologist who is concerned that LDS Social Services' approach is both unprofessional and lacking in the understanding of even basic science.

I am going to speak to you today as a molecular biologist and as someone who sees the world as such. The two points I want to make today is that first, modern research points to the fact, ignored by the Social Services pamphlet, that sexual orientation is biologically and genetically determined. The second point is that what this means is not what most people think it means. It is not a simple dichotomy of "either" or "or" / Nature or nurture. It is much more complex than that. Biology and human behavior can never, ever, be reduced to an "either/or" proposition.

Let me explain to you first why modern research has come to accept that sexual orientation (I speak of sexual orientation, not homosexuality or heterosexuality because that is a false dichotomy, and I'll explain that later) is believed to be genetically and biologically innate and determined. The first is theoretical. Theoretically it is expected to be so.

The Theoretical Approach

Let me walk you through a thought experiment. If you take a population of sexually reproducing organisms with two genders and in that population all the individuals are ambi-

1. Church of Jesus Christ and Latter-Day Saints. Social Services views homosexuality as a mental health problem and offers treatment options.

sexual (a term I made up meaning having no sexual orientation whatsoever), in those individuals, only half of their matings will be successful. If in this population of individuals of ambisexual organisms, you introduce one individual that has a mutation that makes them sexually oriented to only one gender, then every one of that individual's matings will be successful. Over time what happens in a population, a finite population of such organisms, is that that organism's offspring will soon overtake the others and the entire population will be innately sexually oriented.

Another thought in that same thought experiment is to take a population of environmentally determined individuals where in some environments they are heterosexual and in some environments they are homosexual. Again, you can introduce one single individual with one single mutation that makes them innately and irretrievably oriented to only one gender, then sooner or later that population will be innately so. Because almost all the matings of that individual will be successful and all its offspring will carry that gene.

Population Models

There is a basic mathematics population genetic model that every biology student learns. If you take a population and mathematically model it with several versions of a gene (alleles), some of the individuals, if they have offspring, will pass on the gene that gives them 50% male and 50% of their offspring as female and some individuals will have versions of that gene that give them 90% female and 10% of their offspring will be male. What you end up with is that the alleles of those genes work themselves through time over a population, that even if those different genes exist, the entire population will always end up as one half male and one half female.

Now, the reason I bring this up, because it has nothing to do with sexual orientation, is that no matter what population you start out with, all the organisms, end up to be innately sexually oriented. Now once you have such innate, genetic sexual orientation, there are several explanations why homosexuality or bisexuality, or some combination thereof, could be maintained. It could be that the mutation rate that makes a male oriented to a male is higher than the strength of the selection against it in the population, thus maintaining it at a low percentage. It could be a polygenic trait where there are many genes, and many versions of the alleles of that gene that affect the trait. And most combinations of those are advantageous. But, the rare combination causes the individual, or several individuals to be homosexual or such, and that even though that might be considered to be a disadvantage, the advantages of most of the combinations is so overwhelming that it will still persist.

Kin Selection

A third explanation is called kin selection. It is a widely seen phenomenon in birds, insects, mammals and in many other organisms. It can sometimes be advantageous for some individuals to forego reproduction for either all or for some of its lifetime in order to assist their kin to do so. By helping their kin, either their siblings, cousins, or parents to survive and reproduce, they are actually passing on their own genes because their kin are carrying the same genes that they are, including the one that causes them to be non-reproducing, or homosexual in this case.

It is probably most likely that all three of these explanations explain homosexuality from a genetic/biologic point of view.

Now, what we see theoretically, is it true in nature? Well, yes, it is. The fact that sexual desire and orientation have a biological origin in gendered organisms is well substantiated in experiments physiologic, genetic and molecular. It has been found true in a disparate range of organisms from flies to mice. Physiological differences in rats and flies and genetic evidence in flies has shown conclusively that sexual orientation is of biological origin. A recent study in Drosophila (the fruit fly) shows that a misexpression of a gene, called "near the white gene" (because it has other effects), causes male flies to mate with other male flies. The converse is true, that a full expression of this gene causes innate sexual orientation. There is no doubt that sexual orientation in flies and other organisms is genetically determined and thus biological in its origins. This research in organisms and other animals suggests that what we expect theoretically is actually true in nature.

Now it is not always true that what we see in animals is also true in the animal we call human. But, there are two reasons that we might expect that to be true. One is that if we expect it theoretically and then see it in other populations we can reasonably expect to see it in humans. Secondly, if a trait is fundamental, it is expected to be shared among a disparate group of organisms.

Genetic Traits

In the last two decades, researchers have established beyond much doubt that, like high intelligence, green eyes or a propensity for certain diseases, homosexuality runs in some people's genes. Northwestern's J. Michael Bailey, who has conducted much of this research, notes that a male with a gay brother is three to seven times more likely to be gay himself; and a woman with a gay sister is four to eight times likelier to be a lesbian than a female drawn from the broader population.

"The data definitely are not as strong as for other traits such as intelligence or schizophrenia," said Bailey. But he added that researchers from various disciplines are nearing consensus on this point: Some genetic component to homosexuality clearly exists.

Melissa Healy, *Los Angeles Times*, May 21, 2001.

Let me give you a very basic example. There is a protein in all organisms called a "histone" protein. This protein basically binds up your chromosomes into DNA. It is fundamental. There is less than one half of one tenth of one percent of difference between a yeast histone protein and human histone protein. A trait that is fundamental is expected to be shared. A trait such as sexual orientation, which we theoretically believe to be fundamental is expected to be shared. We are now seeing this in humans.

Physiological Evidence

There are physiological differences that recent research has found. Let me quote a common one, Simon Levay's study of the anterior hypothalamus. It is important because, unlike some earlier studies, it looked at a part of the brain that is known to have a function in sexual desire. The difference found in Levay's work, a difference between the size of the anterior hypothalamus between homosexual and heterosexual men, is statistically significant. The work is not without its weaknesses, of course. All homosexual men in his study died of AIDS. The disease could have had, though not shown to have, an effect on the brain's physiology. There are also some concerns that it is not the physiologic differences as the cause of the behavior, but the behavior as the cause of physiological difference.

I am not bringing these evidences up as proof. Science rarely works by proof. It works by a preponderance of evidence in most times, as I have distressingly learned in my research.

Secondly, twin studies. An early twin study in 1956 showed a 100% concordance with the rate of identical twins and a 15% for fraternal twins and homosexuality. This study was admittedly weak, but recent studies by J. Michael Bailey *et al.*, suggest that indeed there is a correlation between homosexuality and relatedness. They found that 50% of all identical twins shared homosexuality. If they were fraternal, the percentage was lower. If they were adopted, the percentage was around 5%. Again twin studies do not prove, but point to the idea that homosexuality is biological in origin.

Recent studies in genetic linkage in humans have shown more conclusively that homosexuality is biological in origin. And sexuality in general. Dean Hamer recently did a study, reported in *Science* in 1993, that there is a linkage on the X chromosome for male sexual orientation. Further studies in his lab have shown the same for female sexual orientation. . . . A [1997] paper [by] Hamer *et al.*, showed a definite linkage for some individuals, a definite genetic origin for homosexuality.

Making Sense of the Science

Now, what does this mean? I am, as a biologist, convinced that sexual orientation is of biological origin. But, this is not what most people think in the popular image of biology or the public debate going on today. It is not an ON/OFF, nature/nurture, gene/no gene event. Even if something is biologic and genetic, it is never determined. . . . Genetic makeup of human beings is never a simple ON/OFF explanation.

There are diseases that are caused by a mutation in a gene.

But, there is something called "penetrance" and sometimes even the mutation does not penetrate to the phenotype (what you see). Let me give a very simplistic analogy. Today we look out at this audience and we see a range of hair color that ranges from blonde to white to black. That range is extreme. Hair color is determined by so many different genes, by pigments, by regulation of pigments, by the very surface of the hair, that we can never tell you what will make a blonde person and what will make a dark haired person. Hair color is also not so easily categorized. You can not say that someone is necessarily blonde because they might be born a towhead, but grow up to be brunette. Someone who has black hair today might be gray tomorrow.

Hair color is not a simple dichotomy. Something as simple as hair color being so complex, you would expect human behavior to be the same. It is of biological origin. But, it is not necessarily the same in every individual. There will be individuals who are innately and irretrievably heterosexual. There will be individuals who are innately and irretrievably homosexual. There will be individuals who are innately and irretrievably bisexual. And, there will be individuals who can change. This is because, even if something is of biologic origin, it is always complex.

Relevance of Biology

In conclusion, I would like to say that the fact that sexual orientation is of biological and innate origin in humans is highly relevant in the ongoing discussion to the church's response to its homosexual brothers and sisters. Some in the church would suggest it is not. Orson Scott Card, a man I respect, and whose writings I love, unfortunately, wrote in an article titled, *The Hypocrites of Homosexuality*: "the argument by the hypocrites of homosexuality that homosexual tendencies are genetically ingrained in some individuals is almost laughably irrelevant."

It would be laughably irrelevant if the actions of the church and its therapists in the past and continuing present hadn't made it so solemnly relevant. It would be laughably irrelevant if the LDS SS and other church counselors hadn't put hundreds of men through tortuous electric shock and aversion therapies to change these children of God. It would be laughably irrelevant if it doesn't force thousands of young men and women through years of fruitless and spiritually debilitating reparative counseling and encourage thousands of men and women into marriage as therapy. I am here to say it is highly relevant whether it is of biological origin or not. Using a simplistic notion, a false dichotomy, and then basing a therapy upon that can only hurt and not help the individuals and children of God.

"Homosexual behavior is learned."

Homosexuality Is Not Biologically Determined

Paul Cameron

According to Paul Cameron in the following viewpoint, homosexuality results from a number of cultural, familial, and social influences. He argues that research claiming a biological origin for homosexuality remains unconvincing. Moreover, Cameron maintains, numerous studies reveal that most homosexuals attribute their sexual orientation to external factors, such as early sexual experiences or absent fathers. Cameron also contends that homosexuals can change their sexual orientation. Cameron is the chairman of the Family Research Institute, a nonprofit educational and scientific corporation.

As you read, consider the following questions:
1. Name the three answers Cameron offers to the question of what causes homosexual urges.
2. In the author's opinion, how does religious conviction affect sexual conduct?
3. What are ex-homosexuals, as defined by the author?

Paul Cameron, "What Causes Homosexual Desire, and Can It Be Changed?" Family Research Institute, 1999. Copyright © 1999 by Family Research Institute. Reproduced by permission.

M ost of us fail to understand why anyone would want to engage in homosexual activity. To the average person, the very idea is either puzzling or repugnant. Indeed, a [1989] survey indicated that only 14% of men and 10% of women imagined that such behavior could hold any "possibility of enjoyment."

The peculiar nature of homosexual desire has led some people to conclude that this urge must be innate: that a certain number of people are "born that way," that sexual preferences cannot be changed or even ended. What does the best research really indicate? Are homosexual proclivities natural or irresistible?

Finding Answers

At least three answers seem possible. The first, the answer of tradition, is as follows: homosexual behavior is a bad habit that people fall into because they are sexually permissive and experimental. This view holds that homosexuals choose their lifestyle as the result of self-indulgence and an unwillingness to play by society rules. The second position is held by a number of psychoanalysts. According to them, homosexual behavior is a mental illness, symptomatic of arrested development. They believe that homosexuals have unnatural or perverse desires as a consequence of poor familial relations in childhood or some other trauma. The third view is "biological" and holds that such desires are genetic or hormonal in origin, and that there is no choice involved and no "childhood trauma" necessary.

Which of these views is most consistent with the facts? Which tells us the most about homosexual behavior and its origins? The answer seems to be that homosexual behavior is learned. The following seven lines of evidence support such a conclusion.

Discounted Studies

Occasionally you may read about a scientific study that suggests that homosexuality is an inherited tendency, but such studies have usually been discounted after careful scrutiny or attempts at replication. No one has found a single heredible genetic, hormonal or physical difference between heterosexuals and homosexuals—at least none that is replicable. While the absence of such a discovery doesn't prove that inherited sexual tendencies aren't possible, it suggests that none has been found because none exists.

Learned Behaviors

Two large studies asked homosexual respondents to explain the origins of their desires and behaviors—how they "got that way." The first of these studies was conducted by Edward Kinsey in the 1940s and involved 1700 homosexuals. The second, in 1970, involved 979 homosexuals. Both were conducted prior to the period when the "gay rights" movement started to politicize the issue of homosexual origins. Both reported essentially the same findings: Homosexuals overwhelmingly believed their feelings and behavior were the result of social or environmental influences.

In a 1983 study conducted by the Family Research Institute (FRI) involving a random sample of 147 homosexuals,

---

Reasons for Sexual Preference

Homosexuality (1940s and 1970)
- early homosexual experience(s) with adults and/or peers— 22%
- homosexual friends/around homosexuals a lot—16%
- poor relationship with mother—15%
- unusual development (was a sissy, artistic, couldn't get along with own sex, tom-boy, et cetera)—15%
- poor relationship with father—14%
- heterosexual partners unavailable—12%
- social ineptitude—9%
- born that way—9%

Heterosexuality (1983)
- I was around heterosexuals a lot—39%
- society teaches heterosexuality and I responded—34%
- born that way—22%
- my parents' marriage was so good I wanted to have what they had—21%
- I tried it and liked it—12%
- childhood heterosexual experiences with peers it was the "in thing" in my crowd—9%
- I was seduced by a heterosexual adult—5%

Paul Cameron, "What Causes Homosexual Desire, and Can It Be Changed?" Family Research Institute, 1999.

35% said their sexual desires were hereditary. Interestingly, almost 80% of the 3,400 heterosexuals in the same study said that their preferences and behavior were learned.

While these results aren't conclusive, they tell something about the very recent tendency to believe that homosexual behavior is inherited or biologic. From the 1930s (when Kinsey started collecting data) to the early 1970s, before a "politically correct" answer emerged, only about 10% of homosexuals claimed they were "born that way." Heterosexuals apparently continue to believe that their behavior is primarily a result of social conditioning.

Older Homosexuals Often Approach the Young

There is evidence that homosexuality, like drug use, is "handed down" from older individuals. The first homosexual encounter is usually initiated by an older person. In separate studies 60%, 64%, and 61% of the respondents claimed that their first partner was someone older who initiated the sexual experience.

How this happens is suggested by a nationwide random study from Britain: 35% of boys and 9% of girls said they were approached for sex by adult homosexuals. Whether for attention, curiosity, or by force, 2% of the boys and 1% of the girls succumbed. In the US, 37% of males and 9% of females reported having been approached for homosexual sex (65% of those doing the inviting were older). Likewise, a study of over 400 London teenagers reported that "for the boys, their first homosexual experience was very likely with someone older: half the boys' first partner were 20 or older; for girls it was 43 percent." A quarter of homosexuals have admitted to sex with children and underaged teens, suggesting the homosexuality is introduced to youngsters the same way other behaviors are learned—by experience.

Early Homosexual Experiences

In the 1980s, scholars examined the early Kinsey data to determine whether or not childhood sexual experiences predicted adult behavior. The results were significant: Homosexual experience in the early years, particularly if it was one's first sexual experience—was a strong predictor of adult homosexual behavior, both for males and females. A similar pattern appeared in the 1970 Kinsey Institute study: there was a strong relationship between those whose first experience was homosexual and those who practiced homosexuality in later life. In the FRI study two-thirds of the boys whose first experience was homosexual engaged in homosexual behavior as adults; 95% of those whose first experience was heterosexual were likewise heterosexual in their adult behavior. A similarly progressive pattern of sexual behavior was reported for females.

It is remarkable that the three largest empirical studies of the question showed essentially the same pattern. A child's first sexual experiences were strongly associated with his or her adult behavior.

Sexual Conduct Is Influenced by Cultural Factors

Kinsey reported "less homosexual activity among devout groups whether they be Protestant, Catholic, or Jewish, and more homosexual activity among religiously less active groups." The 1983 FRI study found those raised in irreligious homes to be over 4 times more likely to become homosexual than those from devout homes. These studies suggest that when people believe strongly that homosexual behavior is immoral, they are significantly less apt to be involved in such activity.

Recently, because of the AIDS epidemic, it has been discovered that, relative to white males, twice as many black males are homosexual and 4 times as many are bisexual. Perhaps it is related to the fact that 62% of black versus 17% of white children are being raised in fatherless homes. But even the worst racist wouldn't suggest that it is due to genetic predisposition.

Were homosexual impulses truly inherited, we should be unable to find differences in homosexual practice due to religious upbringing or racial sub-culture.

Changing Sexual Preferences

In a large random sample 88% of women currently claiming lesbian attraction and 73% of men claiming to currently enjoy homosexual sex, said that they had been sexually aroused by the opposite sex,

- 85% of these "lesbians" and 54% of these "homosexuals" reported sexual relations with someone of the opposite sex in adulthood,
- 67% of lesbians and 54% of homosexuals reported current sexual attraction to the opposite sex, and
- 82% of lesbians and 66% of homosexuals reported having been in love with a member of the opposite sex.

Homosexuals experiment. They feel some normal impulses. Most have been sexually aroused by, had sexual relations with, and even fallen in love with someone of the opposite sex.

Nationwide random samples of 904 men were asked about their sex lives since age 21, and more specifically, in the last year. As the figure reveals, 1.3% reported sex with men in the past year and 5.2% at some time in adulthood. Less than 1% of men had only had sex with men during their lives. And 6 of every 7 who had had sex with men, also reported sex with women.

It's a much different story with inherited characteristics. Race and gender are not optional lifestyles. They remain immutable. The switching and experimentation demonstrated in these two studies identifies homosexuality as a preference, not an inevitability.

Ex-Homosexuals

Many engage in one or two homosexual experiences and never do it again—a pattern reported for a third of the males with homosexual experience in one study. And then there are ex-homosexuals—those who have continued in homosexual liaisons for a number of years and then chose to change not only their habits, but also the object of their desire. Sometimes this alteration occurs as the result of psychotherapy; in others it is prompted by a religious or spiritual conversion. Similar to the kinds of "cures" achieved by drug addicts and alcoholics, these treatments do not always remove homosexual desire or temptation. Whatever the mechanism, in a 1984 study almost 2% of heterosexuals reported that at one time they considered themselves to be homosexual. It is clear that a substantial number of people are reconsidering their sexual preferences at any given time.

What Causes Homosexual Desire?

If homosexual impulses are not inherited, what kinds of influences do cause strong homosexual desires? No one answer is acceptable to all researchers in the field. Important factors, however, seem to fall into four categories. As with so many other odd sexual proclivities, males appear especially susceptible:

1. Homosexual experience:
   - any homosexual experience in childhood, especially if it is a first sexual experience or with an adult
   - any homosexual contact with an adult, particularly with a relative or authority figure (in a random survey, 5% of adult homosexuals vs. 0.8% of heterosexuals reported childhood sexual involvements with elementary or secondary school teachers)
2. Family abnormality, including the following:
   - a dominant, possessive, or rejecting mother
   - an absent, distant, or rejecting father
   - a parent with homosexual proclivities, particularly one who molests a child of the same sex
   - a sibling with homosexual tendencies, particularly one who molests a brother or sister
   - the lack of a religious home environment
   - divorce, which often leads to sexual problems for both the children and the adults
   - parents who model unconventional sex roles
   - condoning homosexuality as a legitimate lifestyle—welcoming homosexuals (e.g., co-workers, friends) into the family circle
3. Unusual sexual experience, particularly in early childhood:
   - precocious or excessive masturbation
   - exposure to pornography in childhood
   - depersonalized sex (e.g., group sex, sex with animals)
   - for girls, sexual interaction with adult males
4. Cultural influences:
   - a visible and socially approved homosexual sub-culture that invites curiosity and encourages exploration
   - pro-homosexual sex education

- openly homosexual authority figures, such as teachers (4% of Kinsey's and 4% of FRI's gays reported that their first homosexual experience was with a teacher)
- societal and legal toleration of homosexual acts
- depictions of homosexuality as normal and/or desirable behavior

Can Homosexuality Be Changed?

Certainly. As noted above, many people have turned away from homosexuality—almost as many people call themselves "gay."

Clearly the easier problem to eliminate is homosexual behavior. Just as many heterosexuals control their desires to engage in premarital or extramarital sex, so some with homosexual desires discipline themselves to abstain from homosexual contact.

One thing seems to stand out: Associations are all-important. Anyone who wants to abstain from homosexual behavior should avoid the company of practicing homosexuals. There are organizations including "ex-gay ministries," designed to help those who wish to reform their conduct. Psychotherapy claims about a 30% cure rate, and religious commitment seems to be the most helpful factor in avoiding homosexual habits.

| "The most effective route to real, lasting change for those caught in same-gender attraction is a redemptive approach."

Homosexuals Can Change Their Sexual Orientation

Sue Bohlin

According to Sue Bohlin in the following viewpoint, homosexuality results when people fail to have their basic human needs met and, in consequence, search for fulfillment in unhealthy ways. She contends that homosexuals can change their sexual orientation through the "redemptive approach." Bohlin maintains that through discipleship, guidance by ministries, and acceptance of God, gays and lesbians can overcome their homosexuality. Bohlin is an associate speaker with Probe Ministries, a nonprofit organization that strives to reestablish Christian values in American society through media, education, and literature.

As you read, consider the following questions:

1. What three treatment options for homosexuality does the author describe?
2. What is the first step toward overcoming homosexuality, according to Bohlin?
3. As reported by the author, what are "ex-ex-gays"?

Mike was marching in a Gay Pride parade when God got a hold of him. He had been high for four days and his "buzz" suddenly evaporated as he heard a voice in his head say, "You don't have to live like this." He knew beyond a shadow of a doubt that it was God offering him a way out. He put down his Gay Pride sign, left the parade, sat down in a nearby stairwell, and repented of his rebellion. He gave his heart to Jesus Christ and started walking out of homosexuality that day. Today, several years later, he is married with a child, and living a very different kind of life. Not just on the outside; his heart was changed from the inside out.

Randy's Story

Randy was on a self-destructive path of drug and alcohol abuse and homosexual activity. When he told his mother he was gay, she threw him out of the house, and the only place he could find belonging, safety, and identity was the gay community. As he spent more and more time "escaping" the pain in his life through sex and alcohol, he began to realize how bad his life was. He wanted to die but God had something else in mind.

Randy was invited to a Bible study where he met a man who had left the gay lifestyle and was living a changed life. For the first time he honestly called out and said, "God, please help me."

One of his friends became a Christian. He asked her about homosexuality and was angered by her initial response. She said, "I now believe it is a sin—but God wouldn't call it a sin if there weren't something better." Randy eventually realized that he was a sinner who needed God's love and grace, and in 1992 he trusted Christ as his Savior. Two months later, he was led to Living Hope, an organization that helps people walk out of homosexuality through an intimate relationship with Jesus Christ. He left his homosexual identity behind and embraced his true identity as a child of God, committed to holiness and purity. Randy is now director of that ministry and is helping others walk out of homosexuality. He's not perfect, he's still growing . . . just like me and every other Christian I know. But the "something better" God had in mind for him is an intimacy with Christ that is breathtaking.

Randy brings glory to God every day of his life by living out the abiding truth that change is possible.

Carol's Story

Carol grew up in a religious home with parents whose standards were too strict to allow her to please them. But she was smart, and a good student, and her teachers gave her the affirmation and encouragement her heart longed for. She developed very strong bonds with her teachers, some of which became profound emotional dependencies.

In graduate school, she was hit by the unexpected pain of loneliness and emptiness. Carol got into an intense relationship with a married woman, facing completely new temptations. She was totally unprepared to resist the strength of same-gender attraction, and quickly found herself emotionally and physically involved in a relationship she couldn't believe was happening. Now she was not only emotionally needy, she was shackled by deep shame, woundedness, and guilt.

A friend told her about a ministry to those dealing with same-sex attraction, and it was like finding a door to another world. Through the support she found there, Carol was challenged to identify the lies of Satan which she had believed her whole life and replace them with the truth of Scripture. God is renewing her mind, meeting her deep heart-needs, and bringing her to a place of freedom and hope.

Diane's Story

Diane's story is different. She spent eighteen years in a committed lesbian relationship with another woman she believed to be her soul-mate. They went through a commitment ceremony in a gay church, and raised a daughter together. She enjoyed a position of leadership as a bright and articulate spokesperson for a gay church.

Through all those years, Diane's mother was steadfast in three things. She loved Diane unconditionally. She never backed down about her belief that her daughter's lifestyle was sinful because God says it's wrong. And third, she prayed faithfully for her daughter.

Diane and her partner sought the Lord about everything except their sexuality. At one point, they were praying together for wisdom and truth about a situation that had nothing to do with their relationship. God answered their prayer in an unexpected way; He showed them the truth about the sinful nature of their relationship. It was a terribly painful and unwelcome discovery to learn that they had been deceived. Together, they decided out of obedience to God to separate and break off their relationship. It's still painful, even as Diane experiences God's healing touch in the deepest parts of her wounded soul. He's changing Diane and Carol from the inside out.

Three Claims for Change

Some people deal with same-sex attraction by pretending it's not there. Denial is unfortunately the time-honored "Christian" response. But this is not the way God wants us to deal with problems; Psalm 51:6 says, "Surely you desire truth in my inmost parts." Acknowledging one has a homosexual orientation is like seeing the red light on your car's dashboard; it means something is wrong somewhere. A homosexual orientation isn't the actual problem; it's the symptom of a deeper issue—legitimate, God-given needs for relationship and intimacy that have been channeled in unhealthy and sinful directions.

But it is not a simple matter, and it would be disrespectful to imply that there is an easy solution to the complex issue of homosexuality. Among those who claim that change is possible, there are three main schools of thought on how to get there.

The first is the deliverance ministries. They say that homosexuality is caused by a demon, and if we can just cast out the demon, the problem is gone. Sounds like an easy fix, but it ends up causing even more problems because homosexuality isn't caused by a demon. The person who was "delivered" may experience a temporary emotional high, but the same temptations and thought patterns that plagued him before are going to return because the root issue wasn't dealt with. Only now, he's burdened by the false guilt of thinking he did something wrong or that he's not good enough for God to "fix" him.

A second and more effective treatment for homosexuality is reparative therapy. There is a lot of wisdom to be found here because many therapists believe that homosexuality has its roots in hurtful relationship patterns, especially with family members, and many homosexual men and women report exactly that. But reparative therapy is often just behavior modification, and it deals only with the flesh, that part of us

How Long Does It Take to Change?

How long the process of change from homosexuality to heterosexuality takes depends on a number of factors. These include:

1. The root issues that are involved. The more difficult or complex the underlying factors involved in a person's same-gender attraction, the longer the process of change may take. For example, the process may take longer for a person who has experienced severe sexual abuse in childhood than for someone who has experienced mild sexual abuse. . . .

2. How much support a person has. The more helpful things a person puts in place, the better progress he or she can expect to make. For example, a woman who only attends the support group will most likely make slower progress than another woman who is also in individual counselling, involved in a church fellowship, and has friends with whom she can share what is happening in her life.

3. One's ability and willingness to face difficult personal issues. As the process of change involves facing difficult personal issues and the pain related to these issues, a person's ability and willingness to face these things will affect their rate of progress. Related to willingness is the question of whether a person truly wants change. Some individuals say they want to change, but are not prepared to take serious steps to accomplish this. A person who thinks, for example, that entertaining a little fantasy now and then is ok, should not be surprised when change doesn't proceed the way they hope.

It is not unusual for the process of change to take 5–10 years. This is no reason to despair. We are not talking about 5–10 years of going through hell! Many people change their identity much sooner than this. Significant relief from the intensity of homosexual feelings can also come much sooner. If God is part of the process, He will walk with you, protect you, direct your path, and shine His light into the darkness. Remember the ultimate goal in life is not heterosexuality versus homosexuality, but following God and giving one's life to Him.

Rob G., *New Direction*, 1999.

independent of God. Reparative therapy can make people feel better, but it can't bring true inner healing.

The Redemptive Approach

The third, and I believe best, way to bring about real and lasting change is a redemptive approach. Ministries that disciple men and women in intimate relationship with Jesus Christ are able to lead them into inner healing because God transforms His people. There are many organizations under the umbrella of Exodus International that provide support and education and discipleship. . . . It's excruciatingly difficult to leave homosexuality without support. Fortunately, even for people who do not live in an area where there is an Exodus referral ministry, there are online support forums that are almost as powerful as face-to-face groups. I especially recommend the one at www.livehope.org. There are also some wonderful books available, particularly *Coming Out of Homosexuality* by Bob Davies, and *Someone I Love Is Gay* by Anita Worthen and Bob Davies. Another excellent book is *You Don't Have to Be Gay* by Jeff Konrad. But discipleship is hard work, and there is no simple and easy fix.

The Path to True Change

The most effective route to real, lasting change for those caught in same-gender attraction is a redemptive approach. This means discipleship, being taught and encouraged and held accountable to develop intimacy with Christ. Interestingly, it doesn't seem to matter what the particular stronghold is in a person's life—whether it be homosexuality, gluttony, drug dependency, compulsive gambling or shopping, alcoholism, sexual addiction, or any other stronghold—the most effective solution is the same: intimacy with Christ.

True discipleship is hard work. And God even gives us the energy for discipleship! But it takes tremendous self-discipline to choose to operate in the Spirit instead of in our own flesh, to depend on God's strength instead of our own. The real battle is in the mind.

The steps to overcoming homosexuality also apply to overcoming any stronghold.

First, the person has to stop the sinful behavior. It's best to ask for God's help. This is no different from the require-ment for any drug or alcohol abuse treatment. You can't work on a problem when you're still totally controlled by it.

The second step is to work on learning what the Bible says about who you are in Christ. Just as people learning to identify counterfeit money examine real currency so they can spot the fakes, the struggler needs to fill his mind with God's Word so he can enter into his true identity as a beloved, valuable child of God.

The third step is working on the thought life, since this is where the battle is. It's important to identify Satan's lies play-ing as tapes in one's head, and stop the tape player! Then, deliberately replace the lies with the truth. Instead of "I'm never going to change," repeat the truthful promise that "I can do all things through Christ who strengthens me" (Philistines 4:13). Instead of obsessing over the aching and longing for the unhealthy and sinful behavior, fill your mind with praise and worship and Scripture.

Next, face the fact that it feels lousy! When we stop try-ing to meet our needs in our own ways, we start experienc-ing the emotional pain that our strongholds had covered up. When it feels really really bad, we are at that very point where God can make the biggest difference. Ask, What is my true need? What is it my heart is truly longing for? Go to Jesus and let Him meet your deepest heart-needs. Let Him direct you to get your divinely-designed needs for rela-tionship with other people met in godly ways.

This is where powerful healing happens.

Ex-Ex-Gays

For the last several years, people who had left homosexual-ity have slowly but surely gained a hearing in telling their stories. Word is getting out: change is possible!

And there are also the voices of the frustrated and disillu-sioned souls who tried to leave homosexuality, who tried to change, and gave up. There's even a name for it: "Ex-ex-gays." Their stories are full of tremendous pain, and some have even lost their faith over it. What happened?

Well, I think the same thing that happened to people who tried AA but couldn't stop drinking, or those who tried Weigh

Down Workshop [a religious weight loss program] but couldn't lose weight. I have a friend who was in Weigh Down Workshop, and it didn't do a thing for her. The problem is, she never made the commitment to "die to self," to use an old spiritual term. She never got to the point of saying, "Jesus, I choose You over food. I choose a holy relationship with You over an unhealthy relationship with my appetite. And I will do whatever it takes to allow You to change my heart."

Many people who tried to change their homosexuality could win contests for praying and reading their Bibles. They really did try very very hard. But the prayers are often misdirected: "God, change me. Take away my desires. Let me start liking people of the opposite sex." Unfortunately, as well-intentioned as this prayer is, it's a lot like trying to get rid of dandelions in your back yard by mowing them. They keep coming back because you're not dealing with their roots. The basic cause of a homosexual orientation isn't genetics or choice; it's a wrong response to being hurt. It's about protecting oneself and trying to get legitimate needs met in ways God never intended. True change can only happen with the hard work of submitting to God, allowing Him to expose the deep hurts and needs of one's heart, which means facing horrible pain, and inviting Him to bring healing to those wounded places. That's why intimacy with Christ is the answer. A wise friend observed that homosexuality is the fruit of sinful ways of dealing with pain—sinful because they cut us off from the One who can heal and meet our needs, sinful because they place us at the center of our universe and we don't belong there. Jesus does.

I hope you can see that real change is hard, and it costs a great deal because it requires strong motivation, hard work, and perseverance. But hundreds of former homosexuals have found a large degree of change, attaining abstinence from homosexual behaviors, lessening of homosexual temptations, strengthening their sense of masculine or feminine identity, correcting distorted styles of relating with members of the same and opposite gender. Some former homosexuals marry and some don't, but marriage is not the measuring stick; spiritual growth and obedience are.

The bottom line is, change is possible.

"[Conversion therapy] harms people and reinforces the notion that homosexuality is bad."

Attempts to Change Sexual Orientation Have Been Unsuccessful

Douglas C. Haldeman

In the following viewpoint Douglas C. Haldeman argues that reparative therapies or conversion programs, designed to change sexual orientation, are ineffective. Moreover, conversion therapies may cause psychological harm to participants, he argues. He maintains that therapists should help homosexuals learn to be comfortable with their sexuality, and society should deconstruct the myth that homosexuality is wrong. Haldeman is the author of *Working with Gay Men and Lesbians in Private Psychotherapy Practice*.

As you read, consider the following questions:

1. According to the author, what does the term "reparative therapy" inaccurately imply?
2. What actions has the American Psychological Association taken to discredit the conversion therapy movement, as noted by the author?
3. In Haldeman's opinion, how does conversion therapy harm homosexuals?

Douglas C. Haldeman, "The Pseudo-science of Sexual Orientation Conversion Therapy," *Angles*, December 1999. Copyright © 1999 by the Institute for Gay and Lesbian Strategic Studies. Reproduced by permission.

Organized mental health declassified homosexuality as a mental illness more than twenty-five years ago. Those who thought this action would mean the demise of therapies designed to change homosexual orientation have only to look at the events of the past year [1999] to realize that some religious political activists and marginalized mental health professionals are seeking to reinstate the "illness" model of homosexuality by peddling the stories of the "cured" to the American public.

Reparative Therapy

As a result of a high-profile advertising campaign promoting treatments for unwanted homosexual orientation, the term "reparative therapy" has become widespread. This term inaccurately implies "broken-ness" as the distinctive feature of homosexuality and bisexuality, however. Since mainstream mental health organizations have rejected this position, the more accurate term for therapeutic efforts to change homosexual orientation is sexual orientation conversion therapy, or simply, conversion therapy.

The promotion of reparative or conversion therapy goes beyond its obvious market of disaffected lesbian, gay and bisexual people. This campaign attempts to influence public opinion and justify anti-gay discrimination by inaccurately portraying homosexuality as a mental disorder and a social evil. Conversion therapy, then, is more than just a clinical issue. It figures prominently in the national debate over lesbian and gay civil rights.

To show why conversion therapy should not influence the development of public policy, this analysis will address several issues:

- Conversion therapy is based on faulty assumptions.
- Homophobia leads some individuals to seek sexual orientation change.
- The mental health professions generally oppose conversion therapy.
- No reliable evidence supports the effectiveness of conversion treatments.
- Conversion therapy can be harmful.
- Conversion therapy adversely affects the public's views of lesbian, gay and bisexual people.

The Faulty Theoretical Foundations of Conversion Therapy

Psychology and psychiatry have no precedents for treating conditions that are not considered to be illnesses. Since 1973 homosexuality has been considered a normal variation of human sexuality. Proponents of conversion therapy disregard this view because of their mistaken belief that homosexuality was declassified as a mental illness only after lobbying from gay activists. The truth, however, rests in the science, or lack thereof, of the "mental illness" assumption of homosexuality.

Homosexuality itself became a mental health diagnosis only as a reflection of prevailing social prejudice. This assumption was first questioned by Evelyn Hooker, who compared matched groups of homosexually- and heterosexually-identified men. She found that scores from psychological tests of the two groups were indistinguishable from one another. Since then, a substantial scientific literature has found no significant differences between homosexual and heterosexual subjects on measures of overall psychological functioning and mental and emotional well-being. The most comprehensive review of such studies was conducted by [researcher J.] Gonsiorek, who also carefully analyzed studies purporting to demonstrate that homosexuality is a mental illness and found them to be rife with methodological problems.

Conversion therapy is based upon the notion that homosexuality is a mental illness and/or a destructive element in society. Theorists such as [Joseph] Nicolosi and [Charles] Socarides maintain that homosexuals suffer from an arrest of normal development. According to their theories, if the circumstances of childhood attachment can be reproduced in therapy, the patient will supposedly overcome his or her homosexuality. Such theories have been described for decades. They have never been empirically validated, however. The theories are concocted from the experiences of unhappy homosexual psychotherapy patients and bear little resemblance to the lives of most lesbian and gay people.

Why People Seek to Change Sexual Orientation

Since conversion therapies operate on the assumption that homosexuality is a mental disorder, conversion therapists assume that they understand why people would wish to change it. No published study of conversion therapy has asked why people would seek to change something as profound and complex as sexual orientation, however. As a result, most conversion therapists incorrectly assume that their clients are motivated by intrinsic negative factors associated with homosexuality, and those therapists ignore the influence of social pressure, which is likely a central factor in individuals' attempts to change their sexual orientation.

Lesbian, gay, and bisexual individuals may be subjected to significant social stress in the form of harassment, violence, and discrimination. These stress factors have been extensively documented, along with their tendency to cause high levels of emotional distress in lesbian, gay, and bisexual people. We do not see a parallel interest on the part of heterosexuals in changing their sexual orientation because they enjoy social privilege. Given that homosexuality is not a mental illness, and in light of the considerable stigma experienced by many gay people, it is likely that people attempt to change their sexual orientation because of the aforementioned social stress factors, as well as pressure from family, society, and church.

[Researcher M.] Yarhouse contends that some people simply find homosexuality at odds with their "values framework" and so freely seek to become heterosexual. But from where do gay, lesbian, and bisexual people derive their "values framework," if not the homophobic world around them? This unsupportive social context is why the argument that people freely seek to change their sexual orientation is unconvincing. Current psychological research on this issue confirms that social factors bear a strong influence on individuals who choose conversion therapy.

The Concerns of Mainstream Mental Health Organizations

The prejudicial and scientifically inaccurate view of homosexuality advanced by conversion therapists has called for a response from mainstream mental health organizations. Historically, most conversion therapy occurred in religious settings, so it was not necessary for mental health groups to comment on the practice. That changed with the emergence of the National Association for Research and Therapy of Homosexuality (NARTH) in the early 1990's. NARTH disseminates material that promotes discredited stereotypes and portrays all lesbian, gay and bisexual people as troubled.

Mainstream mental health organizations in the United States have responded to this challenge. In 1997, the American Psychological Association adopted a policy admonishing all practitioners who deal with lesbian, gay and bisexual clients to refrain from discriminatory practices and from making unscientific claims about their treatments. Therapists must also provide the client with information about the treatment, alternatives, and reasonable outcome expectations. Further, the policy affirms the Association's commitment to the "dissemination of accurate information about sexual orientation," and "opposes portrayals of lesbian/gay/bisexual adults and youth as mentally ill."

In 1998, the American Psychiatric Association took a stronger stand, officially opposing "all forms of therapy based on the assumption that homosexuality per se is a mental illness." Similar policies opposing conversion therapy have been adopted by the American Counseling Association, the National Association of Social Workers, and the American Academy of Pediatrics.

Conversion Therapy's Track Record

Conversion therapists have different views on what constitutes effective treatment. Religious groups often encourage celibacy for their "ex-gay" followers, so lack of sexual contact is construed as successful treatment. Most studies published in the mental health literature use heterosexual behavior as a treatment goal. Much of the effectiveness of conversion therapies is asserted in clients' testimonials or in articles in publications that do not meet accepted research standards. A careful analysis of other evidence of conversion therapy effectiveness fails to justify these recent claims.

The studies that have appeared in legitimate journals are generally quite old and share common methodological problems. Studies of conversion therapy are not based upon a random sample of homosexuals who are randomly assigned to different treatments and are then compared, but on a group of homosexuals who have sought treatment because they are unhappy with their sexual orientation. Furthermore, the studies all rely on clients' self-reported outcomes or on therapists' post-treatment evaluations. As a result, all conversion therapy studies are biased in favor of "cures" because clients of conversion therapy are likely to believe that homosexuality is an undesirable trait to admit and may feel pressure to tell their therapist that the treatment has been successful. Similarly, conversion therapists have an interest in finding that their treatments are successful.

Problems with Classification

The potential for what is known as "social desirability bias" in self-reported outcomes is most obvious in studies of group approaches to conversion therapy. In one group approach, [researcher S.] Hadden finds that 37% of 32 research subjects reported that they had shifted to heterosexuality. But these results must be viewed with skepticism, since therapy groups implicitly encourage individuals to report that they meet the group's standards, even when this is not true.

Misclassification is another widespread flaw in these studies that will inflate reported success rates. Researchers are likely to misclassify bisexual people as homosexual, which makes it more likely that clients will pursue heterosexual behavior even without treatment. A finding that bisexual men can be taught to strengthen their heterosexual behavior is not equivalent to changing sexual orientation. The earliest study attempting to show reversal of homosexual orientation through long-term psychoanalytic intervention reported a 27% success rate in "heterosexual shift." But only 18% of those research subjects were exclusively homosexual to begin with. Fifty percent of the successfully treated men were more appropriately labeled bisexual.

Other studies that report higher success rates share this classification problem. For instance, [researchers P.] Mayerson and [H.] Lief report that half of their 19 subjects were engaging in heterosexual behavior 4.5 years post-treatment. These subjects were actually bisexual going into treatment, however. Exclusively homosexual subjects reported little or no change in that study. Another psychoanalytic study reported virtually no increase in heterosexual behavior in a group of homosexual men. One of the studies used most often to demonstrate that homosexuals can be "changed" was conducted by [researchers W.] Masters and [V.] Johnson. This study also included a number of subjects who were not primarily or exclusively homosexual in their stated orientation, however.

The Importance of Non-Judgmental Therapy

It is our studied belief that the purveyors of "reparative therapy" refuse to confront the underlying reasons for the apparent unhappiness of many of the gay people who seek their help. They presume that all gay people are mentally unwell, ignoring the hundreds of thousands of happy, well-adjusted, successful lesbians and gay men across this nation. At the same time, we believe that human sexuality is a deeply complicated phenomenon that we are not even close to fully understanding. Until then, people need the support of a concerned, nonjudgmental psychotherapeutic establishment to find their own paths, whether they are hetero-, homo- or bisexual.

Kim I. Mills, *Mission Impossible: Why Reparative Therapy and Ex-Gay Ministries Fail*, 1999.

Finally, follow-up of those subjects who meet the subjective criteria for "successful change" in sexual orientation is either poor or nonexistent in conversion therapy studies. Adequate follow-up is likely to uncover cases of reversion to homosexual behavior, which would further reduce the therapy's success rate. [Researcher L.] Birk described a combination-approach group format for treating homosexuality and claimed that 38% of his subjects achieved "solid heterosexual shifts." Nonetheless, he acknowledged that these shifts represented "an adaptation to life, not a metamorphosis," and that homosexual fantasies and activity are ongoing, even for the "happily married" individual. Similarly, a religiously-oriented conversion therapy program described by [researchers E.] Pattison and [M.] Pattison reveals that more than 90% continued to have homosexual fantasies and behavior after treatment.

More comprehensive examinations of conversion therapy studies have been published elsewhere. Those reviews show that no study claiming success for conversion therapy meets the research standards that would support such a claim.

Finally, it should be noted that almost all published research on conversion therapy deals with male homosexuals, not lesbians. Presumably, this reflects a general devaluation of women in clinical research agendas, as well as a greater tolerance on the part of some heterosexual males for lesbians than for gay men. Nevertheless, conversion therapists continue to apply their findings to women, even though their own studies do not support that extension.

The Harm of Conversion Therapy

The studies cited above allege that a typical success rate for conversion therapies is about 30%. Surprisingly, those researchers never question what might have happened to the other 70%. The only comment that conversion therapists offer is that sexual orientation is difficult to change. All conversion therapy rests solidly on the assumption that homosexuality is in conflict with a fulfilling life, balancing out any risks from treatment in the eyes of those therapists. It is important to ask if these treatments might result in negative consequences, however.

This author's fifteen years of clinical experience with gay men who have gone through some form of conversion therapy suggests a wide variability in the way people are affected. All of the following comments are based upon the author's own clinical observations and numerous anecdotal reports which await confirmation in controlled studies.

Some—but not all—conversion therapy clients are harmed. In particular, those who have undergone treatments such as electric shock or drugs inducing vomiting while homoerotic material is presented are likely to have been harmed the most. Many such individuals seen in my practice are not only tormented by an exacerbated level of shame but are physically rendered "asexual"—not changed into heterosexuals, but no longer functioning as homosexuals either.

In recent years, however, refugees from such cruel therapies have become less common in this author's practice as these treatments have fallen into disfavor. At present, the majority of former conversion therapy clients, or "ex-ex-gays", as they are sometimes known, have gone through a religious, prayer-based program or a talk-oriented therapy of some sort. Such individuals often experience continued depression over their homosexuality, compounded with a sense of shame over having failed at conversion therapy. Further, they may have a psychologically debilitating sense of having lost those important life elements—family of origin, religious affiliation, social support—for which there was still some hope as long as the individual was trying to change. Some former conversion therapy clients report extraordinary difficulties with interpersonal interactions, and particularly sexual intimacy, with same-sex partners.

The author's own clinical practice and the views of other practitioners working with former conversion therapy clients suggest that the problems associated with conversion therapy are not limited to the client. The goal of conversion treatments is to involve other individuals in the client's romantic and sexual life. For the ex-spouses and children of conversion therapy "experiment relationships," the sense of betrayal and loss can be devastating. Very often individuals and family members who have been caught in the conversion therapy process need counseling of their own.

The Dangerous Social Implications of Conversion Therapy

The recent conversion therapy ad campaign and the practice of conversion therapy are prime pathways for devaluing lesbian, gay, and bisexual people and reinforcing stigma. Inaccurate information encourages prejudice and discrimination. Research in social psychology tells us that while public opinion about lesbian and gay people has moderated over the past two decades, negative attitudes about homosexuality persist, and lesbian, gay and bisexual people still experience harassment, discrimination, and violence. Although the literature on hate crimes against gay people is only starting to emerge, recent evidence suggests that anti-gay attitudes, fueled by misinformation and cultural sanction, may greatly influence the behavior of those predisposed to abuse lesbian, gay, and bisexual individuals.

But if sexual orientation can be freely chosen, as conversion therapists claim, then why not change it therapeutically? And why pass laws that protect the rights of gay, lesbian, and bisexual people in the same way that laws prohibit discrimination on the basis of race, gender, or national origin? From a practical perspective, even the staunchest advocates of conversion therapy will admit that sexual orientation is extremely difficult to change. For every satisfied client who comes forward claiming that conversion therapy changed her or his sexual orientation, there are many more who disavow its efficacy. Sexual orientation is a deeply rooted, psychologically complex aspect of the human experience. Though one's feelings about his or her sexual orientation may be changeable and susceptible to social influence, no evidence suggests that sexual orientation itself is so malleable.

From a civil rights perspective, the issue of whether homosexuality is unchangeable or a matter of free choice is equally irrelevant. Ultimately, the right of the individual to choose a sexual orientation or to refuse conversion therapy should not be grounds for stigmatization or for limiting civil rights. Our laws provide civil rights protection against discrimination related to numerous characteristics (such as religious beliefs or some disability conditions) that are the product of choices. For instance, 29 states have laws that prohibit discrimination against cigarette smokers.

Conversion therapy is not just an individual mental health issue but has implications for society. This discredited and ineffective psychological treatment harms people and reinforces the notion that homosexuality is bad. In this regard, it is not a compassionate effort to help homosexuals in pain, but a means of exploiting unhappy people and of reinforcing social hostility to homosexuality. Herein lies the real "reparative therapy:" helping refugees of conversion therapy reconstruct their sense of identity and rediscover their capacity to love, as well as repairing a society still affected by the myth that lesbian, gay, and bisexual people are mentally ill. Reparative efforts are best directed toward a broken social context, not the individual who has been victimized by it.

"Straight and gay people have a RIGHT to make choices about their sexual orientation."

Homosexuality Is a Legitimate Choice

Patricia Nell Warren

In the following viewpoint Patricia Nell Warren argues that antigay activists have long insisted that homosexuality is a choice to justify their position that homosexuals can and should become heterosexuals. As a consequence, she contends, many people in the gay community have rejected the idea that they choose to be homosexual. However, according to Warren, all people make choices about their sexuality, such as whether to be homosexual or heterosexual, when and if to come out, or whether to try to change from gay to heterosexual. She maintains that society should respect people's choices about their sexual orientation. Warren is an investigative journalist and novelist who focuses on free speech and gay and lesbian issues.

As you read, consider the following questions:
1. According to the author, why do some church leaders believe that homosexuality is a crime?
2. Why should the APA maintain a neutral position on religious beliefs, in the author's opinion?
3. Name three other controversies over choice described by the author.

"Choice"—and how both gay and religious leaders perceive it—is a key word in today's noisy national debate about gay rights. The issue focuses on the American Psychological Association's (APA) quandary on how it can offer "reparative" therapy [helping gay people become straight] to gay people without seeming to pressure us unduly, or lapsing back into old attitudes that "homosexuals are sick"—or even violating our civil rights.

Today some radical-right church leaders wish to bend APA policy [which denies that homosexuality is a disorder] to their belief that homosexuality is a crime, no different than murder and theft—as per some passages of the Old and New Testament. In their view, gay people SHOULD choose therapy, because they OUGHT to stop being gay. In their view, all therapy should reflect penal law, and all penal law should reflect the Bible.

Rejecting the Idea of Choice

Unfortunately, in their struggle to evade control by this kind of religious thinking, some in the gay community throw the baby out with the bathwater. They reject the idea of "choice." They insist that no choice is involved in sexual orientation . . . that are driven by genes or environmental conditioning or both. "Homosexuals are born, not made," they say.

The fact is, we humans do choose. We make choices about thousands of things, big and small, every day. Choice is what sets us apart from plants and animals. Choice gives us dignity, and allows us to shape our lives, our characters, our destinies.

Even within the gay community, there are landmark choices about how we live and what we do. Choice is involved in the initial decision to overcome fear. "Do I or don't I come out?" No matter what the root cause of homosexuality is, this coming-out decision still confronts us. So does the choice of different scenes—leather, drag. There is the momentous choice to have a sex-change operation. Having unsafe sex with many partners is a dangerous choice. So is the choice to avoid drugs and alcohol as an occasion of unsafe sex. Likewise, a gay or lesbian or bisexual couple who decide to have a loving, monogamous relationship are not operating blindly off natural dynamics. They CHOOSE to live to-gether that way.

Straight and gay people have a RIGHT to make choices about their sexual orientation. This includes the right of some individual gay men or lesbians to leave the Life and seek a "cure"—if that's how they feel. If an individual person decides for whatever reason that they don't feel good living as a homosexual any more—that they want to live as a hetero-sexual, and have all the heterosexual bells and whistles—then they have a right to try to change. After all, their destiny be-longs to them. Their lives are not the property of the gay community or leaders who create our activist rhetoric. Com-munity leaders should not tell people that they HAVE to be gay once they're out. Such pressure turns the gay community into the same kind of prison that the straight world is.

Remaining Neutral

The APA has a duty to the American public to maintain a neutral position on religious beliefs. It should not say to seekers of change that "being gay is bad," or "sick", because this pushes a religious view on all of us. Nor should the APA guarantee the success of "reparative" therapy . . . after all, they can't legally guarantee success of ANY therapy. Today people seek therapy to redirect their lives in many ways—to be more assertive, to be less assertive, to get rid of anger, to find more anger, to take control, to give up control, to be more spiritually sensitive, to come down out of the ether and get more grounded. Therapy operates in all kinds of areas that are not traditionally regarded as "bad" or "sick." Why shouldn't it be the same for sexual orientation?

Private religious organizations that offer private "cures" for gayness—Exodus, Desert Stream Ministries—also have the right to believe as they do about orientation. So until the cows come home, they can go on telling the APA that being gay is bad, and they can offer their own kind of unlicensed help that operates off that belief. But the APA doesn't have to listen to them. Protestant evangelicals have no more right to pressure the APA about the evils of homosexuality than Catholics have to pressure the APA about teachings on Mary. No religion has a right to pressure the APA into a less-than-neutral position on anything.

As to whether choice—therapy or personal will-power—CAN "change" sexual orientation, well—let's get real. We still don't know how orientation is formed, let alone how to change it or defend it from change effectively. Science doesn't yet have a clear fix on this. There is the nature vs. nuture dispute. There is evidence for genetic influence on orientation . . . but there is also evidence of profound social and environmental influence. Yet some activists in the gay community have already built a hard-and fast position on genetics, believing that it's the only workable basis for our rights as a minority group, alongside other minorities who inherit characteristics like gender and skin color.

This seems like a risky choice of tactics to me. Genetics is a slippery slope for such a life-and-death political position—if only because there are variable genes that can kick in at different times of life and change us radically. Genes are volatile things, not cast in bronze, as Nobel prize winner Barbara McClintock discovered. Some minority groups are not based on unchanging lifetime characteristics. Rather, they are built on changeable characteristics—like age. Civil rights protect minors and elders, yet we don't stay in these groups forever. People who are "physically challenged" may not stay that way for a lifetime either, but their rights are protected meantime. Even gender is not immutable, as some transgendered people can tell us.

Based on my own experience and the current state of knowledge, I suspect that orientation may be something innate, but even some innate things are changeable.

Changeable Preferences

Much community rhetoric is based on a concept of immutable bronze-like homosexualness. Many in the community exalt lesbians who have never wanted anyone but women, and men who have never wanted anyone but men. Bisexuals and transgendered people are often made to feel embarrassed and unwelcome because they are viewed as changeable and therefore untrustworthy. Yet in the 20-something years I've been out, I have seen some individual people in the gay community go all kinds of ways in their relationships—from "strictly gay" to "bi," and from "bi" to "hard-core lesbian" and back. Transgendered people are big examples of how people can change. Many gay teens have a very elastic vision of who they are. In real life, the labels don't stick all that well. So community rhetoric and community reality do not always jibe. If some of the community's citizens are that mutable, then a few gay men and lesbians can choose to go straight. And the sky doesn't have to fall because they do it.

The true extent of any "change"—and whether it's real change, or just good camouflage—is a question that goes beyond our ability to observe natural phenomena, into hidden mysteries of the human spirit. The ultimate effects of this kind of "choice" is hidden away in that lonely zone between the conscience of the individual and the Powers of the Universe. Only God and Goddess know if a person really changes . . . or if he or she is just trying to conform to social pressure or religious belief.

Learning About Choice

My own experience taught me much about "choice" in sexual orientation. I knew I was "different" at age 13, despite growing up in the relentlessly heterosexual America of the 1940s. But at age 18, I chose to get married . . . and stayed married for 16 years in an effort to deny my inner reality. In my writing, I chose to ignore the subject of same-sex conflict—or dealt with it in veiled metaphor. My one stab at therapy showed me the harsh judgmental attitudes of therapists in the 1970s (i.e. the therapist believed I was "sick").

After two decades of trying and failing to fit into heterosexuality, I finally chose a different way—that of coming out at age 37. Nobody actually held a gun to my head at any given moment. I had freely chosen to submit to the prevailing heterosexual pressures in our country. And I finally chose to end that submission.

Thirty-seven years of heterosexual indoctrination, and 16 years of experiencing heterosexual sex, did not fundamentally "change" me, in spite of my desperate efforts as both a Protestant and a Catholic to submit my will. Was there something innate in me—natural, genetic—that made me different, and helped me resist change? Whatever it was, it survived. When the prevailing winds bend a young tree long enough, it stays bent . . . but it doesn't change its species. I was still that "different" being who became self-aware at age 13. But two decades of living as an adult heterosexual did powerfully "bend" me and give me the sensibilities of a bisexual. I am not the same kind of person as a young dyke of today, age 13, who discovers her love of females and boldly comes out in junior high and states that she likes only women.

Social Pressures

When we talk about "choice" in sexual orientation, we have to distinguish between a person's freely chosen, deeply abiding, existential sense of "who I am," and a person's choosing to submit to social pressure in order to survive. Over the centuries, many gay men and lesbians and bisexuals were coerced into functioning as heterosexuals, and they fooled everybody—church, family, friends, children, perhaps even themselves. If homosexuality has a genetic basis, then it would seem that these people passed so well because they discovered the power of changing a leopard's spots.

People can be coerced in the opposite direction as well. Extremes of sexual re-conditioning can be seen in American men who go to prison young and spend 10 or 20 years there. When they get out, many are what the activist organization Stop Prison Rape calls "functioning bisexuals." For years, they have conformed to the sex system in men's jails and prisons, which includes "married" cellmates, gang rape of new young inmates, and systematic brutalization of gay inmates. These men were straight when they were first sentenced, but in prison many reach the point where they like sex with men. The film "American Me" gives us a graphic portrait of this type of man.

These grim facts of prison life create a nasty irony for the conservatives and church people who demand that young male criminals be put in adult prisons and punished by longer sentences. On the one hand, prison life shows that some homosexuals and bisexuals can be made, not born. On the other hand, in recent years, our prisons are responsible for massive coercive change in sexual orientation. Today the

U.S.A. has the highest rate of incarceration for young males of any nation in the world. So we shouldn't be surprised to see growing numbers of bisexuals—men who were the victims or perpetrators of savage sexual violence behind bars. When they get out, these men may never "identify" as active members of the gay community. But they may choose to go on seeking sexual and emotional satisfaction with other men, and they may do this in covert, even violent ways.

A similar thing is happening to women, as we send more and more females to prison. Women prisoners are commonly brutalized by male guards. Lesbian relationships are common in prison. In a word, women, too are sexually impacted by the prison experience.

In my opinion, church people should stop screaming so much about "liberal permissiveness" in America today, and take a hard honest look at how their much-loved prisons are re-shaping the sexual destinies of our citizens.

Controversies over Choice

Choices relating to sexual orientation must be seen in context with other controversies about choice. Those who interpret the Bible in a highly authoritarian way hold that we do not own our lives . . . that God owns them, and society owns them as God's representative on Earth. Therefore, according to this view, our right to make certain life-choices ought to be restricted. Some church people argue for greater Biblical control over our society, yet Old Testament law already has a lot of subtle influence on laws that restrict the American "right to choose." When I studied the first five books of the Bible, and saw their powerful influence today on laws regulating everything from youth conduct to cross-dressing, I was illuminated to the Old Testament's role in shaping Western culture.

Juvenile law, for instance. Americans under 18 are commonly denied most rights of adult choice—to make contracts, to refuse medical treatment, to engage in consensual sex, to have free speech. Parents may have children committed to mental institutions at will, or put them in protective custody for the most frivolous reasons, or legally prevent them from running away even when children hate them for their cruelty. These laws have their roots in the Old Testament, where the Law of Moses required a father to kill his children if they disrespected him, disobeyed him or departed from the worship of Jehovah. A girl's virginity was maintained under penalty of death, with her father participating in the execution if she stepped out of line. Even the more recent U.S. child-abuse laws have not prevented some families from cruel expressions of "child ownership." . . .

The Natural Choice

While sexual orientations may not be chosen, in many cases, what behaviors people exhibit in response to their orientations are chosen, and such behaviors can be evaluated morally. A person who by nature, rather than by choice, is more attracted to members of the same sex than the opposite sex still has the choice to recognize and act in accordance with this fact or to repress or act against it. If a person wishes to achieve happiness and promote his life, then he must, in a realm as morally important as sex, act in accordance with his nature. For example, it is morally right for a woman whose nature it is to be sexually attracted to women rather than men to become romantically involved with a woman she loves and desires. In contrast, it is morally wrong for a man whose nature it is to be sexually attracted to women rather than men to become romantically involved with a man rather than seeking out a woman. So there are contexts in which homosexual behavior is immoral (just as there are contexts in which heterosexual behavior is immoral), but there is nothing immoral about homosexuality per se.

Damian Moskovitz, The Objectivist Center, www.objectivistcenter.org, January 5, 2002.

Women's freedom of life choices has certainly been restricted. When I read the Law of Moses passage on a man's duty to kill his wife if she turned away from worship of Jehovah, I understood why we have profound problems with domestic violence today. I also understood why my ex-husband was so obsessed with controlling my thinking, so convinced that he had the right to dispose of my life. Likewise, women are victims of forced therapy in mental institutions, and suffer greater prison penalties for certain crimes, because of culturally ingrained religious belief that their choices should be more restricted.

Last but not least, the authoritarians would deny a woman's right to choose her own life over that of her unborn child—even her right to regulate births. I am fascinated at noticing how the Protestant radical right is joining with Catholicism in militating more and more against simple birth control.

The Suicide Debate

Another big choice involves suicide. The hot discussion about our elders' "right to die" is a reflection of a larger religious belief that suicide is "a crime against God." Of course, some suicides do "evade the law" by succeeding. But in many states, if you fail at suicide, you are punished by incarceration in a mental institution or prison. Why? Because there are powerful people in our society who believe that only God may decide when a human life ends . . . the human has no say in the matter.

Authoritarians face some challenges in their aim to impose the Bible on the choices of all other Americans. Some of us regard the Bible not as the "revealed word of God," but as a collection of sacred and historical writings created by various human writers. It is a document that we all ought to respect, just as the Koran, the Torah, the Bhagavad-Gita, the Book of Mormon, and the Popol Vuh ought to be respected . . . but it's not a document that I or some other Americans would choose to live by the letter of, or want to go to prison because of. Yet some Americans are working to restore the Ten Commandments as a foundation for U.S. penal law and therapeutic practice. If they succeed, then the APA will become a puppet of church politics, and "reparative" therapy will become the law, not a matter of personal choice.

If the United States is to remain a nation where church and state are separated, then we must acknowledge our citizens' right of choice in how each of them perceive their sexual orientation.

Respecting People's Choices

In the long run, it doesn't matter whether orientation is caused by genes or conditioning! What matters is how people choose to declare themselves! Declarations of one's sexual orientation should be respected and protected as fervently as declarations of one's beliefs or politics. And guess what . . . people get to change from Mormon to Catholic, or Protestant to Jew, without losing their human rights. Offering people this choice on orientation doesn't mean (as some church people insist) that we would be opening the door to legalizing bestiality, rape, exploitation of minors, etc. It simply means that, in the area of nonviolent adult consensual relations—if a person decides that he or she wants to "be gay," or wants to "stop being gay," they can make that choice without being unduly pressured by anybody.

Choice is a profoundly human thing that both the straight and gay communities need to acknowledge and dignify in a more realistic way. Gay people shouldn't throw "choice" away just because the radical right have made it one of their buzzwords.

Come to think of it, choice is a sword that cuts both ways. If gay people have the right to choose being straight, then straight people have the right to choose being gay. And maybe some straight people will do just that.

"[Homosexuality] is about . . . loneliness, rejection, affirmation, intimacy, identity, relationships, parenting, self-hatred, gender confusion, and a search for belonging."

Homosexuality Is a Psychological Disorder

James Dobson

In the following viewpoint James Dobson argues that homosexuality is a mental health disorder that can be treated. Parents must be aware of a condition called "pre-homosexuality," he contends, in which children exhibit preferences for clothes, games, and mannerisms that are typically associated with the opposite sex. In addition, inadequate parenting, particularly by the father, can induce homosexual urges in a child, according to Dobson. He maintains that parents should seek therapy early if they perceive signs of pre-homosexuality in their child. Dobson is the founder and president of Focus on the Family, a media and educational organization dedicated to the preservation of the traditional family.

As you read, consider the following questions:

1. Why do pre-homosexual children from Christian homes experience additional pain, according to Dobson?
2. In the author's opinion, why would homosexuals be eliminated from the gene pool if homosexuality were inherited?
3. As stated by Joseph Nicolosi, what are the three A's that effeminate boys yearn for?

James Dobson, *Bringing Up Boys*. Wheaton, IL: Tyndale House, 2001. Copyright © 2001 by James Dobson, Inc. Reproduced by permission.

A few years ago, I received the following scribbled note from a very troubled youth. He wrote:

Dear Dr. Dobson:

I've been putting this off for a long time so I'm finally writing you a letter.

I am a thirteen year old boy. I have listened to your tapes [Preparing for Adolescence] but not the complete set. I did listen to the one on sex though.

Getting to the point, I don't know if I have a serious problem or a passing? (I don't know the word for it).

All through my life (very short) I have acted and look much more like a girl than a boy. When I was little, I would always wear finger nail polish, dresses, and the sort. I also had an older cousin who would take us (little cousins) into his room and show us his genitals.

I'm afraid I have a little sodomy in me. It was very hard for me to write what I just did. I don't want to be homosexual but I'm afraid, very afraid. That was hard to write too. Let me explain further.

Through my higher grades in school (I'm in seventh grade) kids have always called me names (gay, fag etc.), and made fun of me. It's been hard. I have masturbated (I guess) but gone too far. When I was little (not that little) I tried to more than once to suck my own penis (to be frank). That sounds very bad and looks even worse to read it. I pray that nothing is wrong with me.

Very recently I have done such acts as looking (maybe lusting, I pray so hard that I wasn't) at my self in skimpy underwear. Whenever I wear it I feel a like sexual sensation.

Yesterday in the bathroom (in front of the mirror), I wiggled my body very rapidly, making my genitals bounce up and down. I get a little bit of that feeling mentioned above as I write this. After I did this, I immediately asked forgiveness of God, went in the shower but did it again there. I prayed more and felt very bad.

I talked with one of my pastors and told him at that point I probably preferred a man's body over a woman's. Now that was hard to say!

He said he didn't think anything was wrong with me (I don't know how else to say it. He apparently thought it was passing), but I feel very badly and want to know why.

The pastor mentioned above is one I go to for advice very often.

About my spiritual life; I came to Christ only about a year ago but have grown very much. I have also done lot's wrong. I am a Mennonite. What denomination are you? I have been baptized and am well liked in the church (I think).

I'm afraid if I am not straight (that's much easier to write) I will go to hell.

I don't want to be not straight.

I don't try to be not straight.

I love God and want to go to heaven. If something is wrong with me, I want to get rid of it.

Please help me.

Mark

I was deeply touched by Mark's letter. I know him well even though we have never met. He is representative of many other preteens and teens around the world who have awakened to something terrifying within—something they don't understand—something that creates enormous confusion and doubt. These kids often recognize very early in life that they are "different" from other boys. They may cry easily, be less athletic, have an artistic temperament, and dislike the roughhousing that their friends enjoy. Some of them prefer the company of girls, and they may walk, talk, dress, and even "think" effeminately. This, of course, brings rejection and ridicule from the "real boys," who tease them unmercifully and call them "queer," "fag," and "gay." Even when parents are aware of the situation, they typically have no idea how to help. By the time the adolescent hormones kick in during early adolescence, a full-blown gender identity crisis threatens to overwhelm the teenager. This is what Mark was experiencing when he wrote. And it illustrates why even boys with normal heterosexual tendencies are often terrified that they will somehow "turn gay."

Effects of Religion

There is an additional dimension of pain for those who have grown up in a strong Christian home. Their sexual thoughts and feelings produce great waves of guilt accompanied by secret fears of divine retribution. They ask themselves, *How could God love someone as vile as me?* Mark even felt condemned for jumping up and down in the shower and for feeling the excitement it created. (That titillation by the sight of his own body is a classic symptom of narcissism, or a "turning inward" to fulfill his unmet gender-identification needs.) He either had to figure out how to control this monster within or, in his understanding, face an eternity in hell. There is no greater internal turmoil for a Christian boy or girl than this. At the top of Mark's letter he wrote, "I may sound very bad. I hope I'm not that bad."

Poor kid! Mark is in desperate need of professional help, but he is unlikely to get it. His parents apparently don't know about his travail, and the pastor he trusts tells him it will pass. It probably won't! Mark appears to have a condition we might call "prehomosexuality," and unless he and his entire family are guided by someone who knows how to assist, the probabilities are very great that he will go on to experience a homosexual lifestyle.

A Developmental Disorder

There is substantial evidence based on years of clinical experience that homosexuality is a developmental disorder. Every child has a healthy need to identify positively with the parent of the same sex, have same-sex friendships, a positive body image and a confident sexual identity. Homosexual feelings can occur when these needs are not appropriately met. The adolescent's unmet needs become entangled with emerging sexual feelings and produce same-sex attraction. Therapy consists in helping male clients to understand the emotional causes of their attraction and to strengthen their masculine identity. It has been our clinical experience that as these men become more comfortable and confident with their manhood, same-sex attractions resolve or decrease significantly in many patients.

Richard Fitzgibbons, *Washington Times*, January 24, 1997.

What do we know about this disorder? Well first, it *is* a disorder, despite the denials of the American Psychiatric Association. Great political pressure was exerted on this professional organization by gays and lesbians (some of whom are psychiatrists) to declare homosexuality to be "normal." The debate went on for years. Finally, a decision was made in 1973 to remove this condition from their *Diagnostic and Statistical Manual (DSM)*. It was made not on the basis of science but was strongly influenced by a poll of APA members, which was initiated and financed by the National Gay and

Lesbian Task Force. The vote was 5,834 to 3,810. The American Psychological Association soon followed suit. Today, psychologists or psychiatrists who disagree with this politically correct interpretation, or even those who try to help homosexuals change, are subjected to continual harassment and accusations of malpractice.

The second thing we know is that the disorder is not typically "chosen." Homosexuals deeply resent being told that they selected this same-sex inclination in pursuit of sexual excitement or some other motive. It is unfair, and I don't blame them for being irritated by that assumption. Who among us would knowingly choose a path that would result in alienation from family, rejection by friends, disdain from the heterosexual world, exposure to sexually transmitted diseases such as AIDS and tuberculosis, and even a shorter lifespan? No, homosexuality is not "chosen" except in rare circumstances. Instead, bewildered children and adolescents such as Mark find themselves dealing with something they don't even understand.

No Gay Gene

Third, there is no evidence to indicate that homosexuality is inherited, despite everything you may have heard or read to the contrary. There are no respected geneticists in the world today who claim to have found a so-called "gay gene" or other indicators of genetic transmission. This is not to say that there may not be some kind of biological predisposition or an inherited temperament that makes one vulnerable to environmental influences. But efforts to identify such factors have been inconclusive. Despite this lack of evidence, the gay and lesbian organizations and their friends in the mainstream media continue to tell the public that the issue is settled—that gays are "born that way." *Time* and *Newsweek* splashed "promising findings" to that effect on their covers. *Time* titled their story "Search for the Gay Gene," and *Newsweek* proclaimed, "Does DNA Make Some Men Gay?" *Oprah* devoted several slanted television programs to the subject, and Barbara Walters said recently, "There is a growing body of opinion that says that people are born homosexual." Even though entirely false, this politically motivated information (or *dis*information) has done its work. According to a Harris Poll in February 2000, 35 percent of the people polled believed homosexuality was "genetic."

There is further convincing evidence that it is not. For example, since identical twins share the same chromosomal pattern, or DNA, the genetic contributions are exactly the same within each of the pairs. Therefore, if one twin is "born" homosexual, then the other should inevitably have that characteristic too. That is not the case. When one twin is homosexual, the probability is only 50 percent that the other will have the same condition. Something else must be operating.

Furthermore, if homosexuality were specifically inherited, it would tend to be eliminated from the human gene pool because those who have it tend not to reproduce. Any characteristic that is not passed along to the next generation eventually dies with the individual who carries it.

Not only does homosexuality continue to exist in nations around the world, it flourishes in some cultures. If the condition resulted from inherited characteristics, it would be a "constant" across time. Instead, there have been societies through the ages, such as Sodom and Gomorrah and the ancient Greek and Roman empires, where homosexuality reached epidemic proportions. The historical record tells us that those cultures and many others gradually descended into depravity, as the apostle Paul described in Romans 1, resulting in sexual perversion in all its varieties. That ebbing and flowing with the life cycle of cultures is not the way inherited characteristics are expressed in the human family.

Homosexuality Is Treatable

Finally, if homosexuality were genetically transmitted, it would be inevitable, immutable, irresistible, and untreatable. Fortunately, it is not. Prevention is effective. Change is possible. Hope is available. And Christ is in the business of healing. Here again, gay and lesbian organizations and the media have convinced the public that being homosexual is as predetermined as one's race and that nothing can be done about it. That is simply not true. There are eight hundred known former gay and lesbian individuals today who have escaped from the homosexual lifestyle and found wholeness in their newfound heterosexuality. . . .

Psychologist George Rekers says there is considerable evidence that change of sexual orientation is possible—with or without psychiatric intervention. He wrote, "In a sizable number of cases . . . the gender-identity disorder resolves fully."

Dr. Robert L. Spitzer, a psychiatric professor at Columbia University, created a firestorm in May 2001, when he released the results of his research at a meeting of the American Psychiatric Association. Spitzer, who had spearheaded the APA's decision in 1973 to declassify homosexuality as a mental-health disorder, says his findings "show some people can change from gay to straight, and we ought to acknowledge that." This was not what his critics wanted to hear. We applaud Dr. Spitzer for having to courage to examine and then expose the myth of inevitability.

What's Going On?

With that, let's return to Mark's story to explore what is going on within him and other boys who are experiencing prehomosexual urges. We also want to consider what causes their sexual identity disorder and what can be done to help. To get at those issues, we will turn to the very best resource for parents and teachers I have found. It is provided in an outstanding book entitled *Preventing Homosexuality: A Parent's Guide*, written by clinical psychologist Joseph Nicolosi, Ph.D. Dr. Nicolosi is, I, believe, the foremost authority on the prevention and treatment of homosexuality today. His book offers practical advice and a clear-eyed perspective on the antecedents of homosexuality. I wish every parent would read it, especially those who have reason to be concerned about their sons. Its purpose is not to condemn but to educate and encourage moms and dads.

Dr. Nicolosi has permitted me to share some quotes from this book that will answer many questions. These are some of his words:

> There are certain signs of prehomosexuality which are easy to recognize, and the signs come early in the child's life. Most come under the heading of "cross-gender behavior." There are five markets to [diagnose] a child with "gender identity disorder." They are:

1. Repeatedly stated desire to be, or insistence that he or she is, the other sex.
2. In boys, preference for cross-dressing, or simulating female attire. In girls, insistence on wearing only stereotypical masculine clothing.
3. Strong and persistent preference for cross-sexual roles in make-believe play, or persistent fantasies of being the other sex.
4. Intense desire to participate in stereotypical games and pastimes of the other sex.
5. Strong preference for playmates of the other sex.

Cross-Gender Behavior in Children

The onset of most cross-gender behavior occurs during the pre-school years, between the ages of two and four. You needn't worry about occasional cross-dressing. You should become concerned, though, when your little boy continues doing so and, at the same time, begins to acquire some other alarming habits. He may start using his mother's makeup. He may avoid other boys in the neighborhood and their rough-and-tumble activities and prefer being with his sisters instead, who play with dolls and dollhouses. Later he may start speaking in a high-pitched voice. He may affect the exaggerated gestures and even the walk of a girl, or become fascinated with long hair, earrings and scarves. In one study of sixty effeminate boys aged four to eleven, 98 percent of them engaged in cross-dressing, and 83 percent said they wished they had been born a girl.

The fact is, there is a high correlation between feminine behavior in boyhood and adult homosexuality. There are telltale signs of discomfort with . . . boys and deep-seated and disturbing feelings that they [are] different and somehow inferior. And yet parents often miss the warning signs and wait too long to seek help for their children. One reason for this is that they are not being told the truth about their children's gender confusion, and they have no idea what to do about it.

Perhaps you are concerned about your child and his or her "sexual development." Maybe your son or daughter is saying things like, "I must be gay," or "I'm bisexual." You've found same-sex porn in his room or evidence that he has accessed it on the Internet. You've found intimate journal entries about another girl in her diary. The most important message I can offer to you is that there is no such thing as a "gay child" or a "gay teen." [But] left untreated, studies show these boys have a 75 percent chance of becoming homosexual or bisexual?

Distance from Peers

It is important to understand, however, that most of my homosexual clients were not explicitly feminine when they were children. More often, they displayed a "nonmasculinity" that set them painfully apart from other boys: unathletic—somewhat passive, unaggressive and uninterested in rough-and-tumble play. A number of them had traits that could be considered gifts: bright, precocious, social and relational, and artistically talented. These characteristics had one common tendency: they set them apart from their male peers and contributed to a distortion in the development of their normal gender identity.

Because most of these men hadn't been explicitly feminine boys, their parents had not suspected anything was wrong, so they had made no efforts at seeking therapy. Many clients have told me, "If only—back then when I was a child—someone had understood the doubts, the feeling of not belonging—and tried to help me."

But make no mistake. A boy can be sensitive, kind, social, artistic, gentle, and be heterosexual. He can be an artist, an actor, a dancer, a cook, a musician—and heterosexual. These innate artistic skills are "who he is," part of the wonderful range of human abilities, and there's no reason to discourage them. But they can all be developed within the context of normal heterosexual manhood.

In my opinion (and in the opinion of an increasing number of researchers), the father plays an essential role in a boy's normal development as a man. The truth is, Dad is more important than Mom. Mothers make boys. Fathers make men. In infancy, both boys and girls are emotionally attached to the mother. In psychoanalytic language, Mother is the first love object. She meets all her child's primary needs.

Importance of Fathers

Girls can continue to grow in their identification with their mothers. On the other hand, a boy has an additional developmental task—to disidentify from his mother and identify with his father. At this point [beginning about eighteen months], a little boy will not only begin to observe the difference, he must now decide, "Which one am I going to be?" In making this shift in identity, the little boy begins to take his father as a model of masculinity. At this early stage, generally before the age of three, Ralph Greenson observed, the boy decides that he would like to grow up like his father. This is a choice. Implicit in that choice is the decision that he would not like to grow up like his mother. According to Robert Stoller, "The first order of business in being a man is, 'don't be a woman.'"

Meanwhile, the boy's father has to do his part. He needs to mirror and affirm his son's maleness. He can play rough-and-tumble games with his son, in ways that are decidedly different from the games he would play with a little girl. He can help his son learn to throw and catch a ball. He can teach him to pound a square wooden peg into a square hole in a pegboard. He can even take his son with him into the shower, where the boy cannot help but notice that Dad has a penis, just like his, only bigger.

Based on my work with adult homosexuals, I try to avoid the necessity of a long and sometimes painful therapy by encouraging parents, particularly fathers, to affirm their sons' maleness. Parental education, in this area and all others, can prevent a lifetime of unhappiness and a sense of alienation. When boys begin to relate to their fathers, and begin to understand what is exciting, fun and energizing about their fathers, they will learn to accept their own masculinity. They will find a sense of freedom—of power—by being different from their mothers, outgrowmg them as they move into a man's world. If parents encourage their sons in these ways, they will help them develop masculine identities and be well on their way to growing up straight. In 15 years, I have spoken with hundreds of homosexual men. I have never met one who said he had a loving, respectful relationship with his father.

Many of these fathers loved their sons and wanted the best for them, but for whatever reason (perhaps there was a mismatch between the father's and son's temperaments), the boy perceived his father as a negative or inadequate role model. Dad was "not who I am" or "not who I want to be." A boy needs to see his father as confident, self-assured and decisive. He also needs him to be supportive, sensitive and caring. Mom needs to back off a bit. What I mean is, don't smother him. Let him do more things for himself. Don't try to be both Mom and Dad for him. If he has questions, tell him to ask Dad. She should defer to her husband anything that will give him a chance to demonstrate that he is interested in his son—that he isn't rejecting him. . . .

A Blissful Symbiosis

For a variety of reasons, some mothers also have a tendency to prolong their sons' infancy. A mother's intimacy with her son is primal, complete, exclusive; theirs is a powerful bond which can deepen into what psychiatrist Robert Stoller calls a "blissful symbiosis." But the mother may be inclined to hold onto her son in what becomes an unhealthy mutual dependency, especially if she does not have a satisfying, intimate relationship with the boy's father. She can put too much energy into the boy, using him to fulfill her own needs in a way that is not good for him. In reparative therapy [a psychologist's name for treatment of homosexuals], effeminate boys yearn for what is called "the three A's." They are: their father's affection, attention and approval.

If [a father] wants his son to grow up straight, he has to break the mother-son connection that is proper to infancy but not in the boy's interest after the age of three. In this way, the father has to be a model, demonstrating that it is possible for his son to maintain a loving relationship with this woman, his mom, while maintaining his own independence. In this way, the father is a healthy buffer between mother and son.

Recalling the words of psychologist Robert Stoller, he said, "Masculinity is an achievement." [He] meant that growing up straight isn't something that happens. It requires good parenting. It requires societal support. And it takes time. The crucial years are from one and a half to three years old, but the optimal time is before age twelve. Once mothers and fathers recognize the problems their children face, agree to work together to help resolve them, and seek the guidance and expertise of a psychotherapist who believes change is possible, there is great hope.

The Other World

Once again, this short synopsis from Dr. Nicolosi's book is the most insightful material available on the subject. The bottom line is that homosexuality is not primarily about sex. It is about everything else, including loneliness, rejection, affirmation, intimacy, identity, relationships, parenting, self-hatred, gender confusion, and a search for belonging. This explains why the homosexual experience is so intense—and why there is such anger expressed against those who are perceived as disrespecting gays and lesbians or making their experience more painful. I suppose if we who are straight had walked in the shoes of those in that "other world," we would be angry too.

*"Homosexuality . . . is a method of adapting
to adverse circumstances."*

Homosexuality Is Caused by Societal Dysfunction

Jeffrey Satinover

In the following viewpoint, taken from an interview conducted by the National Association for Research and Therapy of Homosexuality, Jeffrey Satinover argues that homosexuality is a way of coping with increasingly negative influences in modern society. He contends that homosexuality should be viewed as a moral and spiritual illness. In Satinover's opinion, homosexuals can—and should—change into heterosexuals. Satinover, a diplomat of the American Board of Psychiatry and Neurology, wrote the book *Homosexuality and the Politics of Truth*. The National Association for Research and Therapy of Homosexuality (NARTH) provides psychological understanding of the cause, treatment, and behavior associated with homosexuality.

As you read, consider the following questions:

1. What examples of intermediate traits does Satinover offer?
2. What example does Satinover give of the "normalization of homosexuality"?
3. According to the author, how is homosexuality a microcosm for common identity problems?

Jeffrey Satinover, "Reflections from Jeffrey Satinover," www.narth.com, September 30, 2002. Copyright © 2002 by the National Association for Research and Therapy of Homosexuality. Reproduced by permission.

The following text is taken from a radio interview in which Dr. Satinover was a guest. He spoke to the interviewer as follows:

In America of late, truth has become subject to terrible political pressure. The question isn't just homosexuality, but rather, freedom from all sexual constraint. This has been an issue for civilization for thousands of years.

Lacking a Moral Compass

I think many people have a sense, especially in America, that too many barriers have come down. We now have so little of a moral compass that we're really completely at sea. We're awash in the tide of unconstrained instinctive behaviors which are all being labeled "okay" because nobody really has a sense, any more, as to what's right and what's wrong. In [mythology expert] Joseph Campbell's words, "Follow your bliss." This has led us into a growing barbarism.

Now we are looking at a generation of young people who are exposed to a sometimes explicit, and sometimes implicit set of values that says that homosexuality is perfectly okay—it's just a complement to heterosexuality.

The implication of such a set of values to an impressionable, possibly confused and certainly exploring youngster, is that there is no reason whatsoever not to go out and try it and see whether it fits. It's simply that a door has been opened and a certain number of people will walk through that door and thereby expose themselves to terrible risks at an age where they are not really capable of making intelligent judgments about the risks.

In the news, now, we're hearing so many overblown claims of a genetic foundation for homosexuality. The whole subject of behavioral genetics is complex. It does not lend itself to sound bites at all.

Genetic Influences

The real genetic question is—what is it in the background of people who become homosexual that opens that door for them, whereas the door is essentially closed for other people?

In a nutshell, every behavioral trait in human nature has a genetic component. For example, basketball playing is clearly genetic. If you were to perform on basketball players the kinds of studies that have been done on homosexuality, you would find an unequivocal genetic association—very powerful, probably much stronger than there is with homosexuality. But if you ask yourself what that's about—it's clear that it's NOT that there is a gene for basketball playing. . . .

The reason there's a genetic association is that there's an *intermediate* trait which allows people who carry these traits to become basketball players in greater numbers than those who do not have those traits—namely, height, athleticism, and so on. So it's not surprising that there is a growing number of studies that show a genetic association to homosexuality. But that is a far cry from saying that homosexuality is genetic in the way that eye color is genetic.

Homosexuality Is Changeable

Of course, there is a political implication to the misuse of the idea that there is a heritable component to homosexuality—that is, the false notion that if it is "genetic," then it must be unchangeable. But I think the most important point that one can make about homosexuality is that it *is* significantly changeable—although statistically, not for everyone.

As a matter of fact, there is an extremely interesting statistic in the more detailed version of the new *Sex in America* survey (*The Social Organization of Sexuality*), which showed that 2.8% of the men in their sample were essentially homosexual. But a much larger percentage had been homosexual at some point in their lives previously. Somewhere between 10% and 16% had apparently gone through a homosexual phase. By gay activist standards they would be people who would have a supposed—and supposedly fixed—"gay identity," yet by the time they were adults and were sampled in the survey, they had given homosexuality up. In fact, the largest proportion by far had given it up.

There are also case reports in the psychiatric literature of single individuals as well as groups of individuals who in a variety of settings actually do spontaneously leave a homosexual identity.

The debate over homosexuality has been profoundly affected by the current culture of complaint. Many, many areas of political life, social life and scientific life today are being profoundly influenced by the various competing claims and cross-claims to victimhood.

A recent article in a psychiatric publication informed us that 30% of all 20-year-old homosexual men will be HIV-positive or dead by the age of thirty. You would think that the objective, ethical medical approach would be: let's use anything that works to try to take these people out of their posture of risk. If it means getting them to wear condoms, fine. If it means getting them to give up anal intercourse, fine. If it means getting them to give up homosexuality, fine. But that last intervention is the one intervention that is absolutely taboo.

There is no doubt that a cold, statistical analysis of this epidemic would lead you to the conclusion that this attitude of political correctness is killing a substantial portion of those people. I think there is an element of denial, in the psychological sense, of what gay-related illnesses really mean.

Normalizing Homosexuality

The normalization of homosexuality was a classic example where the American Psychiatric Association knuckled under to a victim group's pressure tactics. In that instance, no substantive data was presented either to "prove" that homosexuality is an illness, or to "prove" that it is not.

Actually, many of the diagnoses that exist in psychiatry are labeled as illnesses for reasons that have nothing to do with medicine. Instead, psychiatric diagnoses are very subject to intellectual fads that come and go.

The reason the APA talks about disorders—rather than illnesses—is precisely because there are very, very few mental illnesses where underlying pathophysiology is even suspected. In most cases, if you are going to use the term illness, you would have to use it as a metaphor. They are possibly spiritual illnesses, or they are ways of life that are consensually undesirable. But they don't necessarily reflect some underlying disorder in the hardware that backs up the mind.

And so the whole question of what constitutes psychiatric illness is already so weak that it opened the door for activists to come in and make a change in the nomenclature without even having to appeal to rigorous scientific standards. Had they done so, there simply would have been no data one way or another. . . .

National Association for Research and Therapy of Homosexuality (NARTH) Interviews Dr. Satinover

National Association for Research and Therapy of Homosexuality: How did you get involved in the issue of homosexuality?

I had been reading Leanne Payne's *The Healing Presence*. The book describes a sophisticated system of depth psychology from a religious context, where psychological insights are united with healing prayer. After striking up a correspondence with Leanne, I was invited to a conference of hers and I accepted. At that time, I did not even know that the conference was related to homosexuality.

There I met hundreds of people struggling with that issue, and many who had successfully emerged on the other side and were married with children. As I got to know them, I found them to be quite remarkable. The struggle to be healed had left an indelible imprint. I saw a humility, an empathy and a fearlessness about life. They knew exactly what it meant to stand up for what they believed in, since the struggle to become who they truly were had exacted such a cost in suffering.

Eroding Moral Boundaries

If we condone unconstrained sexuality, which seems to be the goal for some of the movers and shakers (so to speak) in our society, and if we continue to advocate tolerance for all behaviors as the only moral value worth retaining, we will ultimately erode what few taboos and moral boundaries are left—including those that protect against incredibly destructive perversions.

Jeff Lindsay, "Homosexuality: Seeing Past the Propaganda," www.jefflindsay.com, November 26, 2000.

The struggle against homosexuality is like so many of the desperate challenges that are common to our modern age—so many people are wrestling with the results of emotional deprivation within the family, because damaged childhoods are so endemic. The life story of a homosexual has parallels for anyone struggling with spiritual, moral and character issues . . . which is to say, all of us!

These people's particular problem happened to be homosexuality, but that was incidental. Their battle was a microcosm for the identity problems of so many people today, who are struggling with what it means to be a man or a woman—with the way that men and women can best relate to one another in the world—as well as with the larger problem of personal identity.

These people had found their way back from the greatest degree of brokenness to embody the values that our culture has always held dear (at least, until recently). They've lived through the most extreme possible crisis and come out the other side. They've wrestled with self-deception to find the truth, and come out with an assurance and self-possession which makes them exemplars of what the therapeutic process ought to produce, but only rarely does. I wanted to be around these people as much as I could, because I knew I had a lot to learn from them.

Homosexuality Was Not Good

Before going to this conference, what had you believed about homosexuality?

I had always been somewhat of an iconoclast and I had therefore been wary of the extent to which the psychiatric profession consistently sold itself out to political fashion on a lot of issues. So I had not bought the PC line entirely. Yet, I was still uncertain. But after meeting these people who were struggling successfully, I realized that to some extent, the wool had been pulled over my eyes by both our culture and the psychiatric profession. Clearly homosexuality was not good, and was changeable. . . .

Should the American Psychiatric Association have de-pathologized homosexuality?

In some ways I think the psychiatric establishment was right—homosexuality is not a disease the way that, say, pneumonia or cancer or schizophrenia are diseases. Homosexuality makes a certain kind of sense as an understandable adaptation to some types of life circumstances. If you grow up in a Cosa Nostra [an American branch of the Mafia] family, it makes sense to be a sociopath. By the same token, it's profoundly confusing to label the sociopathic responses, of, say, war orphans as "disordered" when a war orphan must become a sociopath in order to survive; if he fails to, he may die. So, under the circumstances of war, which response is "healthier"—that is to say, "adaptive"?

Homosexuality, too, is a method of adapting to adverse circumstances. But like sociopathy, it exacts a cost in terms of constrictions in relationships.

So-Called Illnesses

There are many psychological "illnesses" which cannot be adequately or convincingly explained using the medical model of psychiatry. Being homosexual is not like having a tumor. We should throw out the Diagnostic and Statistical Manual and start carefully rethinking all of these so-called illnesses. Right now, the DSM is mostly a collection of problems labeled illnesses because they are simply consensually undesirable within our present culture. But at base, they are *really* issues of values, philosophy, and character.

How can we "prove" to the psychiatric establishment that homosexuality is psychologically unhealthy? When we tried to defend the idea that homosexuality is a disorder as evidenced by the higher associated suicide rate, gay activists said that the suicide was not due to the inherently dissatisfying nature of the condition—it was due to the stresses of homophobia. When we point to the high level of gay promiscuity, they said we were using a narrow, "heterosexist" and outdated definition of promiscuity. Gays could be emotionally faithful to one partner, they argued, while being sexually active with many partners.

And you can't get around those arguments unless you're actually willing to say that promiscuity is an inferior way of life. You need to be able to say that some certain standard is better.

If we can't settle on a shared higher vision, then it's amazing what we must be prepared to accept. For example, there is actually a growing body of literature in sexological journals arguing that the psychological and emotional benefits of promiscuity more than outweigh the risks to life from AIDS.

So that is the fundamental flaw of psychology—it is meaningless without the backdrop of a framework of values.

There I believe homosexuality—like narcissism—is best viewed as a spiritual and moral illness.

Now psychology as a discipline must step up to the table and accept responsibility for the extent to which it has been propagating an amoral ethos. [Fyodor] Dostoevsky put it best in *The Grand Inquisitor*: "Without God, everything is permissible."

Periodical Bibliography

The following articles have been selected to supplement the diverse views presented in this chapter.

Anonymous — "No Easy Victory: An Anonymous Plea from a Christian Husband and Father Who, Day by Day, Resists His Homosexual Desires," *Christianity Today*, March 11, 2002.

Robert Alan Brookey — "Bio-Rhetoric, Background Beliefs, and the Biology of Homosexuality," *Argumentation and Advocacy*, Spring 2001.

David Eidenberg — "It's All in Your Head," *Advocate*, May 26, 1998.

Melissa Healy — "Pieces of the Puzzle: Researchers Are Finding Tantalizing Clues About What Causes Homosexuality and What Signs May Indicate Its Likelihood Early in Life," *Los Angeles Times*, May 21, 2001.

John Marble — "Ex-Gay Pride," *Advocate*, June 5, 2001.

Neil McKenna — "From Limp Wrist to Long Finger," *New Statesman*, April 10, 2000.

Stuart Miller — "It Didn't Work!" *Advocate*, November 24, 1998.

Dahir Mubarak — "Why Are We Gay?" *Advocate*, July 17, 2001.

Richard C. Pillard and J. Michael Bailey — "Human Sexual Orientation Has a Heritable Component," *Human Biology*, April 1998.

Virginia Postrel — "The Claims of Nature: The 'Can Gays Change' Debate Is Muddling the Main Issues," *Reason*, October 1998.

Vernon Rosario — "The 'Gay Gene' Is Born," *Gay & Lesbian Review Worldwide*, September 2001.

Ziauddin Sardar — "The Self-Righteous Gene: Debunking the Notions of a Gay Gene," *New Statesman*, May 24, 1999.

CHAPTER 2

Should Society Encourage Increased Acceptance of Homosexuality?

Chapter Preface

In 2000 the Supreme Court ruled in *Boy Scouts of America vs. Dale* that the Boy Scouts of America (BSA) had the right to exclude homosexuals from being scout leaders. The case overturned a 1999 New Jersey Supreme Court ruling that the dismissal of a gay Scout leader had been illegal under the state's antidiscrimination law. This case is the most recent example of the controversy over whether society should accept homosexuality.

The case was brought by James Dale, who wanted to become a Boy Scout leader after rising to the rank of Eagle Scout, the BSA's highest honor that only 3 percent of Scouts earn. In 1990, after discovering that he was gay, the BSA rejected Dale's application for the adult leadership position and fired him from his job as assistant scoutmaster. The BSA informed him in writing that homosexuality was contrary to the organization's values. Dale sued the Boy Scouts in 1992 under New Jersey's antidiscrimination act, which bars discrimination on the basis of race, national origin, or sexual orientation, among others, in places of "public accommodation." The New Jersey Supreme Court ruled in Dale's favor, contending that the Boy Scouts, with their vast membership and use of public facilities, was not an entirely private organization and therefore must comply with the state's antidiscrimination law. The BSA appealed to the U.S. Supreme Court, who overturned the decision, claiming that the BSA was a private organization that had the right to choose its own leaders and members without government interference.

The Supreme Court decision resulted in a firestorm of controversy between gay activists and advocates of traditional family values. Conservative commentators supported the decision, arguing that the BSA disapproved of homosexual behavior and therefore had the right to reject gay people from their organization. They contended that the organization's stance was clearly and fairly outlined in its 1991 *Position Statement on Homosexuality and the BSA:* "We believe that homosexual conduct is inconsistent with the requirements in the Scout oath that a Scout be morally straight and in the Scout law that a Scout be clean in word and deed, and that homosexuals do not prove a desirable role model for Scouts. . . . As a private membership organization, we believe our right to determine the qualifications of our members and leaders is protected by the Constitution of the United States." Advocates of the Boy Scouts's stance contended that constitutional rights to freedom of association and freedom of speech support the BSA's choice to exclude homosexual leaders and members.

Many others disagreed, maintaining that the BSA's policy violated New Jersey's antidiscrimination law. The American Civil Liberties Union (ACLU) stated, "this case does not involve a right to associate as much as an asserted right to disassociate." The ACLU argued that the Boy Scouts manipulated the right to freedom of association to justify discriminating against a class protected by New Jersey's antidiscrimination law. Freedom of association is typically understood to defend citizens' right to congregate with whomever they choose. However, according to the ACLU, the Boy Scouts's membership is so vast and their recruitment so aggressive that to exclude only homosexuals is blatant discrimination. As stated by the ACLU,

"The exclusionary anti-gay membership policy that the Boy Scouts now so vigorously defends falls outside the scope of any associational or expressive freedom protected by the First Amendment."

The issue of whether the BSA should be forced to accept gay leaders and members reflects the larger social problems of exclusion and discrimination. Many people argue that the important question is not whether certain groups have a right to freedom of association but how to lessen society's desire to disassociate from homosexuals or any other minority group. As stated by dissenting Superior Court justice Robert L. Stephens regarding the *Dale* decision, "That such prejudices are still prevalent and that they have caused serious and tangible harm . . . are established matters of fact." Stephens and others maintain that upholding the right to discriminate hinders progress toward an unbiased community.

Authors in the following chapter debate society's attitudes concerning the acceptance of homosexuality. As the Dale decision illustrates, the issue generates vociferous debate between those who disapprove of homosexuality and those who argue for increased tolerance of gays and lesbians.

"[Homosexuals] are simply asking to engage in monogamous, non-incestuous relationships with people they love."

Society Should Accept Homosexuality

John Corvino

In the following viewpoint John Corvino contends that arguments grouping homosexual relationships with polygamous, incestuous, and bestial relationships are unfair. He argues that there is no logical connection between these different relationships and to group them together ignores the complexity of human intimacy. Homosexual relationships offer partners the same means of interpersonal communication and fulfillment that heterosexual relationships do, he maintains, and therefore should be accepted. Corvino teaches philosophy at Wayne State University in Michigan and is the editor of *Same Sex: Debating the Ethics, Science, and Culture of Homosexuality.*

As you read, consider the following questions:

1. According to Corvino, what is a good reason to abandon the "we really exist" argument?
2. Why is polygamy troublesome for traditionalists, in the author's opinion?
3. Why does Corvino consider the bestiality analogy particularly annoying?

S ome bad arguments never die. Consider, for example, the argument that the approval of homosexuality is tantamount to the approval of polygamy, bestiality, and incest. This argument made news again recently when the notorious [radio personality] Dr. Laura used it in response to the [2000] Vermont decision [to grant the privileges of marriage to homosexual couples—termed civil unions]. "If two men can be sanctified in this country as marriage," she asked, "then what is your logical or justifiable reason to exclude adult incest? A man and a woman—consensual, 25 years old, who are brother and sister—should not be discriminated against because they have a genetic relationship."

Dr. Laura's argument is nothing new, having been used against interracial marriage until the 1960's. Once you begin tinkering with the institution of marriage, the argument goes, you start down a slippery slope with no reasonable stopping point. But what Dr. Laura's argument lacks in originality it makes up for in rhetorical force, or so it would seem: Given the choice between rejecting homosexuality or accepting a sexual free-for-all, most Americans are inclined to opt for the former.

Unfortunately, sound-bite arguments don't always lend themselves to sound-bite refutations—which is one reason why they're so appealing. Part of the problem is that the polygamy/incest/bestiality (PIB for short) argument is not so much an argument as it is a challenge to sexual liberals to explain why polygamy, incest, and bestiality are wrong. Most people are not prepared to do that—certainly not in twenty words or less. And the answers that come to mind—for example, that PIB relationships violate well-established social norms—won't work as a defense of same-sex relationships, since they too violate social norms.

In what follows I attempt to respond to the PIB argument. I am particularly concerned here with the moral issue: Does the approval of gay and lesbian relationships commit one to the approval of polygamous, incestuous, or bestial relationships from a moral standpoint? One might also approach this as a public policy issue: does legalization of gay marriage lend support for legalization of any of the other types? Indeed, Dr. Laura's version of the argument seems aimed in that direction: Still, the public policy issue is separate from the moral issue in this debate.

Two Inadequate Responses

Let me first address two popular responses that I think are inadequate. The first argues that homosexuality is different from polygamy, incest, and bestiality because homosexuality can be "constitutional" to some individuals, while the same is not true of polygamy, incest, or bestiality. Call this the "We really exist" argument. As [journalist] Andrew Sullivan writes,

> Almost everyone seems to accept, even if they find homosexuality morally troublesome, that it occupies a deeper level of human consciousness than a polygamous impulse. Even the Catholic Church, which believes that homosexuality is an "objective disorder," concedes that it is a profound element of human identity. . . . [P]olygamy is an activity, whereas both homosexuality and heterosexuality are states.

Sullivan is probably right in his description of popular consciousness about homosexuality. Yet traditionalists may reject the idea that homosexuality is an immutable condition of the person. At a June 1997 conference at Georgetown University, "Homosexuality and American Public Life," conservative columnist Maggie Gallagher urged her audience to stop thinking of homosexuality as an inevitable, key feature of an individual's personality. Drawing on the work of queer theorists, ironically enough, Gallagher proposed instead that homosexuality is a cultural construction—one that ought to be challenged.

Of course, pace Gallagher, the fact that homosexuality is socially constructed does not entail that it is easily changed—as David Halperin explained in an interview . . . in *One Hundred Years of Homosexuality:*

> Just because my sexuality is an artifact of cultural processes doesn't mean I'm not stuck with it. Particular cultures are contingent, but the personal identifies and forms of erotic life that take shape within the horizons of those cultures are not. To say that sexuality is learned is not to say that it can be unlearned—any more than to say that my culture changes is to say that it is malleable.

Halperin is right to distinguish the essentialist-versus-constructionist debate from what we might call the voluntarist-versus-non-voluntarist debate on the (im)mutability of homosexuality. But traditionalists might grant that homosexuality is in some cases immutable and still refuse to acknowledge that it's a deep and important feature of personality. Moreover, many traditionalists—including Dr. Laura— outspokenly endorse "reparative" therapy for homosexuals, and would thus reject Sullivan's premise about homosexuality being an inalterable state as opposed to a chosen activity.

Whether or not homosexuality is deeply rooted or unalterable, there are good reasons for abandoning the argument that "We really exist." For one thing, it sounds dangerously close to "We just can't help it." What's more, the rebuttal to this argument is all too obvious: "Alcoholics really exist, too; they can't help their impulses either—but we don't encourage them." Of course, one could respond that the effects of alcoholism are quite different from those of homosexuality. But such an argument is not to the point, which is that demonstrating that a characteristic is deep or immutable is not tantamount to demonstrating that is desirable to have or act upon.

The Equal Options Argument

A second response to the PIB challenge is to argue that as long as PIB relationships are forbidden for heterosexuals, they should be forbidden for homosexuals as well. Call this the "equal options" argument. To put the argument more positively: homosexuals are not asking to engage in polygamy, incest, or bestiality. They are simply asking to engage in monogamous, non-incestuous relationships with people they love—just as heterosexuals do. As [columnist] Jonathan Rauch writes:

> The hidden assumption of the argument which brackets gay marriage with polygamous or incestuous marriage is that homosexuals want the right to marry anyone they fall for. But, of course, heterosexuals are currently denied that right. They cannot marry their immediate family or all their sex partners. What homosexuals are asking for is the right to marry, not anybody they love, but somebody they love, which is not at all the same thing.

This argument, too, is correct as far as it goes, but it doesn't go far enough to satisfy proponents of the PIB argument. As they see it, permitting homosexuality—even monogamous, non-incestuous, non-bestial homosexuality—involves relaxing some traditional sexual mores. The fact that these mores prohibit constitutional homosexuals from marrying somebody they love is no more troubling to traditionalists than the fact that these mores prohibit, say, constitutional pedophiles from marrying somebody they love, since traditionalists believe that there are good reasons for both prohibitions.

In short, both arguments are vulnerable to counterexamples: alcoholics really exist, and pedophiles are denied equal marital options. Indeed, as traditionalists are fond of pointing out, homosexuals do have "equal" options, strictly speaking: they can marry their choice of opposite-sex partner just as heterosexuals can. (Traditionalists usually remain silent on whether this option would be a good idea for anyone involved.)

Another Approach

There is, I think, a better response to the PIB argument, one that has been briefly suggested by both Sullivan and Rauch (whose contributions to this debate I gratefully acknowledge). It is to deny that arguments for homosexual relationships offer any real support for PIB relationships. Why would proponents of the PIB argument think otherwise? Perhaps it's because they misunderstand the central argument in favor of homosexual relationships. They think the central justification is simply that some people want such a relationship, presumably because it makes them feel good; and if it's consensual, why not? If that were all there were to the argument, then it would indeed offer support for PIB relationships. But it is a straw man.

Most defenses of homosexuality have proceeded by examining and refuting various objections to homosexual relationships. Missing is any substantial development of a strong argument in favor of homosexual relationships. So I begin by offering such an argument. A homosexual relationship, like any sexual relationship, can unite two people in a way that ordinary friendship cannot. It can be an avenue of growth, of communication, and of lasting interpersonal fulfillment. These are some reasons why heterosexual people have sexual relationships even if they can't have children or aren't trying to procreate (which is probably most of the time). And if these are morally sufficient reasons for non-procreating heterosexuals to have sex, they should be morally sufficient reasons for homosexuals to have sex.

Traditionalists have several possible responses here. They can bite the bullet and begin condemning non-procreative heterosexual sex. Needless to say, few will take this route. They can argue that homosexual relationships lack the benefits of non-procreative heterosexual relationships. While some (notably John Finnis) have attempted this argument, their efforts are unconvincing. Finnis, for example, appeals to a vague and embarrassingly ad hoc notion of "the marital good" in an attempt to distinguish homosexual relationships from non-procreative heterosexual ones. More plausibly, traditionalists can argue that despite the initial similarities, there are some morally relevant differences. Space considerations prohibit me from exploring such arguments and possible responses here. Suffice it to say that there is a strong prima facie case for treating homosexual and heterosexual relationships as morally, socially, and politically the same.

Understanding Homophobia

Gay people have gained unprecedented rights and respect in recent decades, but homophobia continues to fuel moral reform movements on the right and exerts influence center court. Sometimes our obsession with other people's sexual orientations seems second only to our obsession with race. It's baffling. I understand gossip and prurience, but not moral outrage or even concern about the sexual preferences of consenting adults. Homophobia can't simply be attributed to religion (there is considerable support for gay rights in some religious communities), although it is often cloaked in religious rhetoric. But fear and loathing of gay people does seem as visceral as love of God, and equally tenacious.

Wendy Kaminer, *American Prospect*, February 28, 2000.

"But wait," say the opponents. "Can't you make the same argument for PIB relationships?" Not quite. It's true that you can use the same form of argument, to wit: PIB relationships have benefits X, Y, and Z and no relevant drawbacks. But whether PIB relationships do in fact have such benefits and lack such drawbacks is another matter, one that will not be settled by looking to homosexual relationships. To put the point more directly: to observe that many people flourish in homosexual relationships is not to prove that others might flourish in incestuous, bestial, or polygamous ones. Whether they would or not is a separate question—one that requires a whole new set of data.

Illogical Groupings

Another—and perhaps more efficient—way to indicate the logical distance between homosexual and PIB relationships is to point out that the latter can be either homosexual or heterosexual. Proponents of the PIB challenge must therefore explain why they group PIB relationships with homosexual relationships rather than heterosexual ones. There's only one plausible reason: PIB and homosexuality have traditionally been condemned. But that's also true of interracial relationships, which traditionalists (typically) no longer condemn. And they've just argued in a circle: the question at hand is why we should group PIB relationships with homosexual ones rather than with heterosexual ones. Saying that "we've always grouped them that way" begs the question. Why should they be grouped that way in the first place? What in essence do they all have in common?

Here it may be worth returning to the question of whether PIB relationships can be said to carry benefits sufficient to warrant their approval. Answering that question requires far more data than I can marshal here. It also requires careful attention to various distinctions, such as the difference between morality and public policy, or between the morally permissible and the morally ideal. Also, the three elements of PIB, polygamy, incest, and bestiality, are as different from each other as each is from homosexuality. Let me offer some brief (and admittedly inconclusive) observations about each of these phenomena.

Polygamy provides perhaps the best opportunity of the three for obtaining the requisite data: There have been and continue to be numerous polygamous societies worldwide. The vast majority are polygynous societies, in which one man is allowed more than one wife. Such societies tend to be strongly male-dominated, and it's an open question whether an egalitarian sexual order is even possible under polygamy. Nevertheless, it seems plausible that some people might flourish under polygamous social arrangements. Polygamy is also troublesome for traditionalists in that it has biblical support. True, the Bible reports troublesome jealousies among the sons of various wives, which perhaps should be taken as a lesson. But polygamy is clearly a case in which traditionalists can't point to "God's eternal law." Moreover, at least one of the arguments typically offered against homosexual marriage, that it's bad for children, may actually work in favor of polygamous marriage.

Some have argued that the principle that prohibits both homosexual and polygamous relationships is based on the "teleology of the body." Only one man and one woman can produce a new life: homosexual relationships are inadequate to this goal, and polygamous relationships are superfluous. Yet one can easily acknowledge that producing children is good without inferring from this fact that not producing children is bad. Moreover, numerous medieval philosophers, including St. Thomas Aquinas, noted that the teleology of the body is consistent with polygyny, since it is in the nature of the body that one man can easily impregnate more than one woman.

Incestuous Relationships

Incest comprises a wide variety of practices. In our own society incest—especially between an adult and a child—is linked to various harms, both physical and psychological. But recall that Dr. Laura's example involved "a man and a woman, consensual, 25 years old, who are brother and sister"—thus circumventing some of the standard objections. One might raise the possibility of birth defects, but that argument collapses in the homosexual case. Can I produce an argument to demonstrate that adult consensual homosexual incest is wrong? Not in twenty words or less. A longer argument might explore the delicacy of family bonds. But the important thing to remember is that it's not incumbent upon the defender of homosexuality to produce such an argument. If there are good arguments against such a relationship, they will remain unaffected by the argument in favor of homosexuality.

The analogy with bestiality is the most annoying of the three. To compare a homosexual encounter—even a so-called "casual" one—with humping a sheep is to ignore the distinctively human capacities that sexual relationships can (and usually do) involve. It is to reduce sex to its purely physical components—precisely what traditionalists are fond of accusing gay rights advocates of doing. That noted, claiming that bestial relationships are qualitatively different from human homosexual relationships does not prove that bestial relationships are immoral. Nor does the lack of mutual consent, since we generally don't seek consent in our dealings with animals. No cow consented to become my shoes, for example. Upon reflection (and I've given this issue more thought than I care to admit), I feel about bestiality much as I feel about sex with inflatable dolls: I don't recommend making a habit out of it, and it's not something I'd care to do myself, but it's hardly worthy of serious moral attention.

All told, the PIB challenge is longer on rhetorical flourish than on philosophical cogency. There is no logical connection between any of the four phenomena. Why, then, do traditionalists continue to put forth this red herring? Perhaps it's because they've run out of genuinely plausible arguments against homosexuality, and so now they're grasping at straws. And then there's the emotional factor. Mentioning homosexuality won't make people squeamish the way it once did, but mentioning bestiality and incest will at least raise some eyebrows, if not turn some stomachs. Dr. Laura and her ilk know they're losing the cultural war against homosexuality, and they're trying to change the subject. We should steadfastly refuse to let them.

"The homosexual revolution seeks to destroy
. . . the divinely ordained family."

Society Should Not Accept Homosexuality

William Norman Grigg

New American senior editor William Norman Grigg argues in the following viewpoint that homosexuality, which was once spoken of only behind closed doors, has become a part of mainstream culture. The "gay agenda," he alleges, has permeated the workplace, public schools, movies, television, and politics. He contends that the "Lavender Revolution" must be stopped because homosexuals seek to usurp the traditional family.

As you read, consider the following questions:

1. According to Grigg, why was Rolf Szabo fired from his job?
2. Why is Richard Hatch's *Survivor* triumph representative of the "Lavender Revolution's" cultural advance, in Grigg's opinion?
3. As described by the author, what was the first stage in Marshall Kirk and Hunter Madsen's plan to manipulate society into accepting homosexuality?

William Norman Grigg, "Unmentionable Vice Goes Mainstream," *New American*, vol. 18, November 18, 2002, pp. 8–14. Copyright © 2002 by New American. Reproduced by permission.

Is it possible that someday it may be a crime to oppose homosexuality? Could the Holy Bible eventually be designated "hate literature," and preachers be accused of "hate crimes" for condemning the practice from their pulpits? Will parents be forbidden to teach their children to abhor homosexuality? This all seems improbable, or even impossible—but as the case of Rolf Szabo illustrates, the homosexual movement now has the power to punish those unwilling to "celebrate" that lifestyle.

Rolf Szabo's Story

Prior to his firing in October [2002], Rolf Szabo had worked for Eastman Kodak for 23 years. By all accounts Szabo, a resident of Greece, New York, was a capable and conscientious employee. But Szabo discovered that under the new workplace dogma of "diversity," job performance is less important than displaying correct attitudes.

In early October, according to Rochester ABC television affiliate WOKR, "Kodak's diversity group sent out an e-mail asking employees to 'be supportive' of colleagues who choose to come out on Gay and Lesbian Coming-Out Day." Replying to the message, Szabo tersely told Kodak's sensitivity commissars to stop sending him emails that he considered "disgusting and offensive." "I don't need this to do my job," Szabo explained. "It has nothing to do with gay [issues]. It could have been any other topic. It's just that enough is enough. We really don't need this to do our jobs."

According to Szabo, Kodak officials demanded that he sign a letter renouncing his "homophobic" attitudes. When he refused he was fired. "The Eastman Kodak Company gives me a paycheck; they don't own me," Szabo told WOKR. "I'll go somewhere else for a paycheck, that's all."

Gay-Friendly Policies

While extreme, Szabo's experience is not unique. "Diversity groups" like Kodak's are now a standard feature for many major corporations. Corporate workshops and seminars intended to encourage "sensitivity" regarding homosexuality are becoming commonplace, and those who climb the corporate ladder frequently find that advancement depends as much on their supposedly progressive attitudes as it does on their education, abilities, and performance. . . .

"I think the main issue lies in a corporate organization trying to force people to believe certain things with mandatory-type seminars and workshops," commented a Motorola employee in an August [2002] wire service interview. Speaking anonymously, the individual criticized the global electronics firm for imposing a series of mandatory "Homophobia in the Workplace" workshops. An employee at the Palo Alto headquarters of the Hewlett-Packard computer firm told *The New American* that the corporation similarly emphasizes "promoting inclusion." The individual cited a recent corporate newsletter that warned: "Any comments or conduct relating to a person's race, gender, religion, disability, age, sexual orientation, or ethnic background that fail to respect the dignity and feeling of the individual are unacceptable."

"Diversity training is becoming mandatory catechism class for the church of the politically correct," notes Attorney Jordan Lorence of the Alliance Defense Fund. In post-modern America, it's not enough merely to tolerate homosexuality and similar perversions; these destructive vices must be embraced in the name of "celebrating diversity." As Rolf Szabo can testify, "non-discrimination" policies intended to make workplaces "gay-friendly" can lead to unemployment for non-conformists—a sobering consideration for professionals trying to find traction in tough economic times. Many Americans who espouse traditional moral views disapprove of homosexuality but prefer a "live and let live" approach. But Szabo's case offers just one of numerous illustrations that partisans of the homosexual revolution aren't willing to respect that proposed cease-fire in the culture war. . . .

Targeting the Youth

Homosexual change agents in the corporate world insist that the battle against workplace "discrimination" must include indoctrinating straight employees regarding the evils of "homophobia." In government-run schools across the nation, even more aggressive efforts to indoctrinate schoolchildren are carried out in the name of preventing classroom "harassment" and combating youth suicide.

This strategy was pioneered in Massachusetts by the Boston-based Gay, Lesbian and Straight Educators Network (GLSEN). According to GLSEN's Kevin Jennings, homosexual activists "seized upon the opponent's calling card—safety—and explained how homophobia represents a threat to students' safety by creating a climate where violence, name-calling, health problems, and suicide are common." Jennings and subversives of his ilk insist that "gay" teens account for up to one-third of all teen suicides, often driven to self-destruction by feelings of rejection and loneliness. While it's true that serious behavioral disorders like homosexuality can breed suicidal tendencies, the off-cited truism linking teen suicide to "homophobia" is entirely bogus.

In January 1989, the Department of Health and Human Services (HHS) published a four-volume report dealing with teen suicide. Attached to the report's findings was a brief polemical essay entitled "Gay Male and Lesbian Suicide," written by Paul Gibson, an obscure San Francisco social worker. Gibson blamed the traditional family and conventional religion for the problems experienced by suicidal homosexual youth. He described religion as a "risk factor in gay youth suicide because of the depiction of homosexuality as a sin and the reliance of families on the church for understanding homosexuality." Gibson's essay specifically targeted "traditional (e.g., Catholic) and fundamentalist (e.g., Evangelical) faiths [which] still portray homosexuality as morally wrong or evil."

The HHS included Gibson's essay despite a lack of documentary evidence to support its astonishing claims. This lent the federal government's prestige—such as it is—to the homosexual lobby's contention that traditional family life and orthodox religion are enemies of the public good, since they supposedly contribute to the risk of teen suicide.

This spurious linkage inspired a February 1993 report from the Massachusetts governor's office entitled *Making Schools Safe for Gay and Lesbian Youth: Breaking the Silence in Schools and Families*. It required that "all certified teachers and educators will receive training in issues relevant to the needs and problems faced by gay and lesbian youth. Such training should be a requirement for teacher certification and school accreditation." Two years later, GLSEN appeared on the scene with a program to "educate" parents and communities about homosexuality, using teen suicide as a wedge issue. "In Massachusetts, no one could speak up against our frame and say, 'Why, yes, I do think students should kill themselves'; this allowed us to set the terms for the debate," observes Jennings. This strategy "automatically threw our opponents onto the defensive and stole their best line of attack."

Consequently, many Massachusetts public school students are subjected to homosexual indoctrination, often involving shockingly explicit discussion of depraved sexual practices. And the objective is to begin indoctrinating children at the earliest possible age.

Having worked with the Massachusetts Governor's Advisory Commission on Gay and Lesbian Youth, Karen Harbeck insists "by seventh grade it's too late. People say this is an issue mainly for high school sex education class. They're wrong; it belongs in pre-school."

High school students in Kensington, Massachusetts, were assigned to read a textbook claiming that sexual activities may be "less threatening in the early teens with people of your own sex" and that "growing up means rejecting the values of your parents." Students in a middle school in Ashland, Massachusetts, were assigned "gay" parts in a role-playing exercise about "discrimination." Two boys were compelled to act the role of a homosexual "couple" seeking to adopt a child; one of them was forced to utter the line, "It's natural to be attracted to the same sex.". . .

Permeating Popular Culture

Unless they are determined to withdraw from public life, Americans simply cannot avoid the subject of homosexuality and its offshoots. Lavender Revolution propaganda has literally saturated our nation's popular culture.

Scores of recent major films depict homosexuals as veritable saints, exploiting the mainstream appeal of unambiguously masculine leading men by casting them in homosexual roles. Dennis Quaid, who earned the gratitude and respect of mainstream audiences in early 2002 for his role in *The*

Rookie, offers a useful example. *The Rookie* was an unabashedly pro-family, pro-Christian film based on the true story of a middle-aged schoolteacher and baseball coach who made it to the big leagues. In two other recent films—*Frequency* and a remake of *The Parent Trap*—Quaid convincingly played admirable characters devoted to family. However, [in the winter of 2002], on the heels of these crowd-pleasing offerings, Quaid stars in *Far from Heaven*, playing "a 1950s suburban husband tormented by his inability to control his homosexual longings," in the words of the homosexually themed *Advocate* magazine.

Singling Out Homosexuals

Homosexuality . . . is only one of many ways of life that are not right or healthy. I do not wish to Bible thump, but there is much wisdom in the Bible. For example: "Do you not know that wrongdoers will not inherit the kingdom of God? Do not be deceived! Fornicators, idolaters, adulterers, male prostitutes, sodomites, thieves, the greedy, drunkards, revilers, robbers—none of these will inherit the kingdom of God." Homosexuality is only one of many types of behavior condemned in the Bible.

Obviously, we all are guilty of sinful behavior and yet are accepted as part of society. Why single out the gay community for nonacceptance? I think the only reason is that none of the other behaviors listed above have proponents trying to claim such behavior is OK when it is not. Only the gay community has such a lobby, and most people are turned off by the selling job. Most people do not care what others do; just do not ask for approval of it. . . .

Why are not gays accepted by most of society? To be accepted by respectful society, you must behave in a respectful manner. Stop promoting your lifestyle as something healthy and good; stop pushing your agenda in our schools; stop public displays of sex; condemn organizations like NAMBLA [North American Man/Boy Love Association].

John C. LeDoux, *Roanoke Times & World News*, July 7, 2002.

Similarly, the 1994 homosexual agitprop film *Philadelphia* cast Tom Hanks—an actor whose immense box office appeal was built around his everyman screen persona—as a mild-mannered homosexual dying from AIDS. Tom Selleck, who played macho Vietnam vet-turned-Private Investigator Thomas Magnum on television for eight seasons, played a homosexual reporter in the 1998 film *In & Out*, a role that called for him to kiss actor Kevin Kline on-screen. Since 1987, British Shakespearean Patrick Stewart has lent his resonant baritone and regal bearing to *Star Trek*'s heroic Captain Jean-Luc Picard—with a brief detour as a flamboyantly "gay" interior designer in the 1995 AIDS "message film" *Jeffrey*. James Gandolfini took a brief sabbatical from playing a tough, womanizing mafia don on HBO's *The Sopranos* to play a macho homosexual hit man in the Julia Roberts/ Brad Pitt romantic comedy *The Mexican*.

Why would such roles in often less-than-successful films attract such bankable stars? "Hollywood has a way of whipping people into line, of making them 'team players' and conform to a politically correct message," observes Dr. Ted Baehr of the Christian Film and Television Commission. Dr. Baehr told *The New American* that "there is great pressure brought to bear [in Hollywood] on some actors and creative people who are well-intentioned, church-going people who are made to believe that embracing 'diversity' regarding homosexuality is the key to winning the respect of the industry, and a way to make the world a better place. And the power brokers have ways of torturing people—through professional and personal ostracism, or other retaliation—to bring them to heel.". . .

Conquering Television

It is difficult to overstate the impact of the Lavender Revolution's conquest of prime-time television. The year 1995 marked a watershed in that campaign, according to the *Orange County Register.* That "was the year that Gay Came to Stay on prime-time TV," noted the newspaper. "Suddenly, gayness was cool. Although gay characters still weren't allowed to connect physically in prime time, homosexuality became a topic open for discussion on series old and new." And characters of all sexual persuasions pattered about it. . . . [Almost ten] years later, "you can scarcely find a TV show without a sympathetic lesbian or gay character," ecstatically observed lesbian activist E.J. Graff in the October

21, 2002, issue of *American Prospect*.

The viewing public has also embraced homosexual characters who are somewhat less than sympathetic. In 2000, tens of millions of American television viewers tuned in to learn the winner of the first installment of *Survivor*, a "lifeboat exercise"[1] disguised as a game show.

The contestant who claimed the $1,000,000 prize was Richard Hatch, an openly homosexual "corporate trainer" who prevailed over his rivals through psychological manipulation—an object lesson tragically ignored by the show's vast audience. According to several news accounts, the victorious Hatch received an avalanche of marriage proposals from both male and female viewers.

Psychological Warfare

Richard Hatch's *Survivor* triumph is uncannily representative of the Lavender Revolution's cultural advance, which is also the result of sophisticated psychological manipulation—so sophisticated that most Americans have little concept of the scope and rapidity with which the unmentionable vice has gone mainstream.

"Between 1987 and 1993—the dates of two exhilarating and massive gay-rights marches on Washington—lesbian and gay issues were dragged out of the Ann Landers and home decor columns and onto the front and editorial pages, where they have remained," writes E.J. Graff in her *American Prospect* essay. "Perhaps the most important is the change in lesbians' and gay men's daily lives: Mentioning a same-sex partner in ordinary conversation—to co-workers, doctors, nurses, teachers, contractors, strangers on a plane—no longer feels death-defying. . . ."

Although Graff makes no mention of a book entitled *After the Ball: How America Will Conquer Its Fear and Hatred of Gays in the '90s*, by Marshall Kirk and Hunter Madsen, her essay serves as a postcript to that "Gay Revolution" manifesto. Nearly a decade ago, *The New American* described the campaign laid out in that book, designed to use the mass me-

1. Used in a classroom setting as a form of psychological conditioning, "lifeboat settings" typically place participants in a disaster scenario in which their survival depends on consigning others to death.

dia to condition the public to accept and support the homosexual cultural revolution.

In their revolutionary blueprint, Kirk and Madsen outline a carefully calibrated campaign to "convert" society in a fashion congenial to homosexuality. "By conversion . . . we mean conversion of the average American's emotions, mind and will, through a planned psychological attack," they write. "We mean 'subverting' the mechanism of prejudice to our own ends—using the very process that made America hate us to turn their hatred into warm regard—whether they like it or not."

The Process of Conversion

The first stage of the process outlined by Kirk and Madsen is to make the subject of homosexuality ubiquitous. "At least at the outset [of the campaign], we seek desensitization and nothing more," they write. "You can forget about trying right up front to persuade folks that homosexuality is a good thing. But if you can get them to think it is just another thing—meriting no more than a shrug of the shoulders—then your battle for legal and social rights is virtually won." One key objective was simply to make the previously unmentionable subject unavoidable: "The fastest way to convince straights that homosexuality is commonplace is to get a lot of people talking about the subject in a neutral or supportive way."

Once this is achieved, continue Kirk and Madsen, it would be necessary to "portray gays as victims, not as aggressive challengers. . . . Gays must be cast as victims in need of protection so that straights will be inclined by reflex to assume the role of protector." Graff aptly illustrates that tactic by describing the saturation coverage provided to the [1998] death of homosexual activist Matthew Shepard in Wyoming, dishonestly portrayed as an anti-homosexual "hate crime." (It was actually a brutal robbery-murder that had no demonstrated connection to Shepard's lifestyle.) Because of the media's focus on the Shepard murder and other supposed "hate crimes," explains Kevin Cathcart of the Lambda Legal Defense and Education Fund, "The definition of what shocks the conscience has changed"—meaning that it is now opposition to homosexuality, rather than the vice itself, that is supposedly considered shocking.

Shepard has practically become an icon. During the 2002 Miss America Pageant, Miss Nevada, Teresa Benitez, recited a letter written by Shepard's father and read by him in court to one of his son's murderers. And "conservative" Oregon Republican Senator Gordon H. Smith featured Shepard and his mother Judy in television ads during his reelection campaign. "My son Matthew was viciously murdered simply because he was gay," intones Mrs. Shepard. "Gordon Smith stands with me in the fight against hate. Matthew would have liked Gordon a lot."

That a "conservative" Republican would conscript the ghost of a homosexual activist as a character reference tellingly illustrates where we are as a society.

The Next Phase

Drawing on the Kirk/Madsen battle plan, once the public has been properly "desensitized," "conditioned," and "converted," attention must be turned on individuals and institutions that simply won't conform to the program. At this point, notes *After the Ball*, "it will be time to get tough. To be blunt, [traditionalists] must be vilified. . . . The public should be shown images of ranting homophobes whose secondary traits and beliefs disgust middle America. These images might include: the Ku Klux Klan demanding that gays be burned alive or [tortured]; bigoted southern ministers drooling with hysterical hatred to a degree that looks both comical and deranged. . . ."

The hate-saturated caricatures thus described are difficult to avoid in movies, television, and in what is offered by that branch of the entertainment media that calls itself the "news." The product of this pervasive indoctrination is evident in Rolf Szabo's case, and in the way some schoolchildren feel obligated to denigrate their parents as homophobes.

And the revolution, according to Graff, has just begun. While much "progress" has been made, she contends, "it's not yet time for the forces of justice to abandon the field; the gay and lesbian cultural victory is still pretty limited." Homosexuals have yet to conquer such institutions as the military, the Boy Scouts, and marriage—but she's hopeful that homosexuals, "with enough help from our progressive friends," will ultimately prevail on those battlegrounds as well.

The "progressive friends" Graff alludes to are deployed as change agents throughout our society, conducting a long march through our institutions. Following a blueprint laid down by Italian Communist theorist Antonio Gramsci, these subversives are seeking to capture the culture, thereby eradicating all institutional impediments for creating the Total State. Writing in the Winter 1996 issue of the Marxist journal *Dissent*, Michael Walzer took stock of the Gramscian revolution's progress. Among the victories won by cultural Marxists in the "Gramscian war of position," is "the transformation of family life," particularly "the emergence of gay rights politics, and . . . the attention paid to it in the media."

The homosexual revolution seeks to destroy, through lethal redefinition, the central institution of a free society—the divinely ordained family. This is why the Gramscian change agents have made the Lavender Revolution a priority—and why that revolution's designs must be actively opposed.

> "How we understand homosexuality in our culture and how this reflects our values, beliefs and world view has tremendous educational value."

Schools Should Stress Acceptance of Homosexuality

Kevin Jennings

According to Kevin Jennings in the following viewpoint, teaching acceptance of homosexuality in schools is crucial. Homosexuality is an important issue that children deal with on a daily basis, he argues. Jennings maintains that teaching students about homosexuality will help them learn to think critically about social issues. Jennings is the executive director of the Gay, Lesbian, and Straight Education Network.

As you read, consider the following questions:
1. What does the author believe constitutes a good education?
2. According to Jennings, what fueled the growth of public education in the late nineteenth century?
3. What, in the author's opinion, is a threat to children?

Kevin Jennings, "What Does Homosexuality Have to Do with Education?" *GLSEN Education Department Resource*, January 1, 1999. Copyright © 1999 by the Gay, Lesbian, and Straight Education Network. Reproduced by permission.

The Radical Right is increasingly targeting gays in general, and gay issues in education in particular, as part of an overall strategy to impose their vision of America on the rest of the country. They have been able to play on the fears of many well-meaning people to advance this agenda. The basic worry of every parent is, "Is my kid safe?" By playing on the myth that homosexuals recruit children, reactionary attacks on inclusive education direct a positive impulse—the desire to have the best for one's children—toward a destructive end—intolerance for others.

Trouble in Merrimack

This became poignantly clear to me when I traveled to Merrimack, New Hampshire in August [1998]. Townspeople in Merrimack were fighting an anti-gay policy being put forth by some reactionary board members, a policy that would ban any representation of gay issues in a positive or even a neutral light. At the request of local organizers, I came to Merrimack to speak at a rally being held the night the school board was set to vote on the policy.

I arrived early so I could observe the school board debate. Perhaps because I was wearing a tie, a mother in her mid-thirties standing near me decided I must be on her side of an argument that had divided the large audience in attendance, the bulk of whom seemed to be against the policy's passage. She sidled over to me and began to unload her frustration with what she saw as a foreign issue that had no place in her town's schools. Saying all she wanted was "pure education" for her children, she finally exploded. "What does homosexuality have to do with education?" she demanded.

The setting didn't allow me to fully answer her provocative and important question, so it has stayed with me. What does homosexuality have to do with education, after all?

A Good Education

To answer her question, we have to first answer another: What is a good education? For me, education is about learning to think. A good teacher is one that takes a subject that matters to his or her students and helps them to think about it in a thoughtful, critical manner. In America, we have also traditionally seen the opportunity to get an education as the first step on the road to success, and created the world's first free public school system to make sure that all people got an equal chance to develop the critical faculties that are the product of a good education. Good public education is an essential part of a democracy where the citizens rule and are free to advance themselves as far as their abilities, ambitions and hard work will take them.

Homosexuality itself has nothing to do with education, any more than biology, chemistry, algebra or any other subject does. What is important is what one can learn from the study of a given subject. A discussion of how we understand homosexuality in our culture and how this reflects our values, beliefs and world view has tremendous educational value. It is clearly a subject that matters to kids: they talk about it, they ask about it, they use phrases like "That's so gay" routinely, so few can argue that it isn't a subject that needs addressing (although some will, believe me!). The question is, can we use it to help students think and learn? The answer is manifestly yes.

But this is not the agenda of folks who put forth policies like that passed in Merrimack on August 14, [1998]. They see education serving a different purpose. For them, schools are there to inculcate values: developing independent thought is not the overriding goal. And they call upon a strong historic tradition in this belief. The vast growth of public education in late nineteenth century America was fueled, at least in part, by the fears of native whites who saw the influx of southern and eastern European immigrants as a threat to their way of life. They saw the public schools as means to "Americanize" these foreign elements and to indoctrinate them with "American values."

The "Gay Agenda"

Today, many families feel bewildered by the rapid cultural change sweeping our nation, and some have been led to believe that a "gay agenda" is, at least in part, responsible for what they see as a breakdown of our society and a seemingly-bleak future for their children. They feel that if they can regain some sense of control over what goes on in their community's schools, maybe the whole society will become a little more coherent. They often just want to feel as if things are not completely out of control. So they come out to public meetings and demand to know what homosexuality has to do with education, and demand that it be banished so that the schools can return to the basics of reading, 'riting, and 'rithmetic.

Slurs in School

Anti-LGBT [lesbian, gay, bisexual, and transgendered] slurs have become the insult of choice whether the targeted student is in fact LGBT, perceived to be, or heterosexual. A host of recent studies affirm this fact, demonstrate the pervasiveness of anti-LGBT slurs in schools, and confirm the power of words to wound:

- 88% of the 1,000 students interviewed in a 2001 national phone survey conducted by Hamilton College reported having heard classmates use "gay" as a derogatory term

- 4 out of 5 students in the 1999 Safe Schools Coalition survey who said that they had experienced anti-LGBT harassment (80%) identified as heterosexual

- According to *Hostile Hallways: Bullying, Teasing, and Sexual Harassment in School*, a 2001 study conducted by the American Association of University Women (AAUW), 73% of students would be "very upset" if someone said they were gay or lesbian. Among boys, no other type of sexual harassment, including physical abuse, provoked so strong a reaction.

Nancy Goldstein, "Zero Indifference: A How-To Guide for Ending Name-Calling in Schools," www.glsen.org, 2001.

Sadly these people are pawns in a game, a game wherein unscrupulous politicos manipulate their very real and legitimate concerns for short-term political gain. Those doing the manipulating cleverly fly the banner of "parental control." They protest that they have nothing against gays—Merrimack school board members who voted for the policy in question repeatedly said they were not prejudiced and would not tolerate verbal gay-bashing in their schools—but that they only wish to make sure that parents have the final say over what their children learn. Who could be against that?

It will do no good to point out the illogic of this position. Parents have little say over the day-to-day teachings of a

school, and any school where they did would quickly become an unmanageable bureaucratic nightmare. Imagine if
every lesson plan had to be approved by parents before implemented—nothing would get taught at all while we attended interminable board hearings. Parental control is only
invoked when a particular subset of parents wants to impose
their own values on a school.

Speaking to Parents' Fears

Pointing this out, however, would have had little effect on
the mother with whom I spoke in Merrimack. She had real
fears about her children, and wanted them addressed. Knowing this, we must start thinking now about how to speak to
her fears. We must help her understand that an education
that teaches her children to think for themselves, rather than
one that turns them into automatons, is her best hope for securing their future in the global marketplace. We must help
her understand that bigotry and name-calling represent a
greater threat to her child's welfare than an open discussion
of touchy issues. We must help her understand that silencing people will never make an issue go away, but will simply
cause it to fester.

In short, we must help her understand that homosexuality
is not a threat to her children: homophobia is.

That is what homosexuality has do to with education. It's
about freedom of thought, it's about the ability to use one's
mind, it's about the right to be educated rather than trained.
And we have to help people who don't understand that to
get it.

"Religious freedom and freedom of speech issues are threatened by programs [that encourage acceptance of homosexuality]."

Schools Should Not Stress Acceptance of Homosexuality

Linda P. Harvey

In the following viewpoint Linda P. Harvey argues that teaching students about homosexuality in schools exposes children to a risky and unhealthy lifestyle. She contends that homosexual advocacy groups claim to promote a safe environment for homosexual students at school. In reality, in Harvey's opinion, homosexual activists strive to eliminate all opposition to homosexuality in schools, thereby silencing traditional viewpoints. Harvey is president of Choice For Truth, an organization dedicated to fighting pro-choice and pro-homosexual sentiment in society.

As you read, consider the following questions:

1. What are two erroneous assumptions made by homosexual activists, according to Harvey?
2. What messages do students get when educators pair gay issues with genuine civil rights issues, in the author's opinion?
3. As stated by the author, what punishment does GLSEN recommend for children who make derogatory statements about homosexuals?

At Woodbury High School near St. Paul, Minnesota [in 2001], inverted pink triangles were placed in fifty classrooms and offices. The purpose of the symbol, students were told, was to designate so-called "safe" locations where students could discuss same sex attractions with a teacher or counselor. Students were promised these discussions would be free from any disapproval of homosexual, bisexual or transgendered behavior. The campaign was instigated by the principal and a school librarian without the knowledge of either the school board or the PTA. It was only after a brave student wore a T-shirt to school bearing the slogan "Straight Pride" that a controversy ensued and the whole program was revealed. What was also revealed was that a simple, non-violent expression of support for heterosexuality was not "safe" for that student—because he was suspended.

The Safety Ploy

This new selective notion of "safety" is a favorite ploy of groups like GLSEN (the Gay Lesbian and Straight Education Network) and PFLAG (Parents and Friends of Lesbians and Gays). In fact, at Woodbury High School, students who request one of these private, "safe" conversations about homosexuality are often referred to the local chapter of PFLAG or a local homosexual youth group. No parental permission or notification is required for these referrals. Through this clever plan, students are introduced to homosexuals and possibly put on a fast track into that lifestyle before a parent knows what's happening.

Both GLSEN and PFLAG have worked diligently for years to construct an acceptable front for familiarizing adolescents and children with homosexual behavior. They say they want to help troubled students, so they advance a shaky vehicle called "safety" which plays well with parents concerned about their offspring. I believe that many PFLAG and GLSEN volunteers sincerely believe this, misguided though they are. They claim that homosexuality is harmless and an inevitable identity for certain teens and even small children. But facts don't support their beliefs. This Trojan Horse is based on four erroneous assumptions:

1. Homosexuality is no more harmful than any other sexual behavior.
2. Homosexuality is an unchangeable identity and even a civil rights issue.
3. Society's emphasis on heterosexuality and traditional marriage is discriminatory and an obstacle to homosexual rights.
4. Any objection to homosexuality quickly leads to violence, and those who object can be lumped into a catch-all group with racial bigots.

Protecting Against Lawsuits

School districts across the country are being pressured by civil liberties groups to adopt both "non-discrimination" and "anti-harassment" policies. Citing federal law about overall "sexual harassment," the American Civil Liberties Union (ACLU) and others lead school districts to believe that they must specifically use the term "sexual orientation" in these policies or they are open to suits.

Present conduct codes that all schools have in place aren't enough, the civil liberties groups say. Schools must do more to create the desired "safe" climate for homosexual, bisexual or cross-dressing students. The question one must ask is, what is the desired outcome of "safety" here? Are we talking about protection from the biggest of bullies, or from outright assault?

No, we need to look at the rest of the story. A "safe" school is one that is free from any objections to homosexuality, in the fondest dreams of homosexual activists. That includes moral, health, or religious concerns, or simply finding the behavior distasteful. Until one understands this, the real goals aren't clear. In order to escape the wrath of these activists, the ACLU, Lambda Legal Defense Fund and all the other allies, *schools must de-emphasize heterosexuality* and traditional marriage, and do everything possible to silence traditional viewpoints.

To show they aren't "discriminating," schools must prove their loyalty by starting homosexual clubs for students; teaching about famous people who are claimed to have been homosexual; teaching about alternative families, including those headed by two homosexuals; and using so-called "inclusive" language and material that excludes the terms "husband," "wife," "boyfriend," "girlfriend" and so on.

GLSEN's own materials recommend teaching all students the importance of legalizing marriage for homosexuals and fighting this thing called "heterosexism." Why are we seeing recommended reading lists in middle and high schools now that are full of everything but traditional families? It's because of pressure from feminists joined with "gay" activists. [2001's] reading list at our local high school included stories about homosexuality, of course; but also family drug abuse, alcoholic parents, suicide, and so on. The darkest and weirdest will become the norm—anything to escape the conventional.

Holding High Schools Hostage

Statistics on school violence are *decreasing*, despite the tragic school shootings of recent years. The American Medical Association released a study showing that school violence is down. Even so, GLSEN, PFLAG and others claim that widespread bullying of homosexual students is on the rise, and that schools just aren't doing enough about it. Holding schools hostage to their unique definition of "safety," schools must cooperatively set aside "safe zones" designated by pink triangles, and hold school-wide events like "days of diversity" or "days of silence." Homosexual "coming out" days in October, or "gay pride" events in the spring are also common demands of activist teachers, staff and students who are members of homosexual clubs. Such activities are said to increase support and acceptance of homosexuals, implying of course that this is a fixed identity, not a risky and avoidable behavior.

But as far as these groups are concerned, the debate is over. Heterosexuality is now just plain old "offensive," as student Elliott Chambers found out in Minnesota. To these totally indoctrinated school officials and students, it is seen as hostile action and a "safety" issue. Woodbury High School's actions in suspending him resulted in a lawsuit, where Elliott's parents claimed First Amendment discrimination. The U.S court in Minnesota recently ruled in favor of the Chambers' case.

Woodbury High School is not alone. Increasingly, schools

are initiating similar discriminatory programs. One reason is that there is federal money available for this instruction. I'm referring to the Safe and Drug Free Schools Program, Title IV of the Elementary and Secondary Education Act, the [2002] "No Child Left Behind" Act, which provides millions of dollars to educators to develop lessons and hire staff to combat drugs and violence. The section of the program devoted to education about prejudice, intolerance and hate crimes goes beyond racial and religious tolerance to also include the category of "sexual orientation."

The brochure outlining the violence education portion of the Safe and Drug Free Schools program is called "Preventing Youth Hate Crime." That publication says, (and I quote): "Prejudice and the resulting violence can be reduced or even eliminated by instilling in children an appreciation and respect for each other's differences." As the program is further described, we learn that some of the "differences" they want our children to learn to "respect" include homosexual, bisexual and transgendered behavior. In the resources section of this federally-funded publication, PFLAG and another homosexual advocacy group are listed. No resources are listed which hold that homosexuality might be a problem for our children. . . .

Healing the Hate

A curriculum called "Healing the Hate" was recently developed with funding from the Safe and Drug Free Schools program. It teaches middle schoolers about the Holocaust, lynchings, church burnings, and hate groups. Gays and lesbians need protection from such groups, too, this curriculum teaches sixth, seventh and eighth graders. In one classroom exercise, each student is given a slip of paper describing an incident of discrimination that actually occurred. Each student is to read his or her example. Out of the 58 hate incidents included, 12 involve homosexuals. As a former teacher of eighth graders, it is clear to me that the takeaway for students this age will be sympathy toward all homosexuals as victims. Clearly, that is the program's intent. And—I feel I must apologize to the rest of America for the contribution my state's senator, Ohio's Mike De Wine, made by taking a leading role in constructing the "Safe and Drug Free Schools" program.

But we're not just talking about assault here. Two of the incidents cited in this exercise involve speech only. This falls in line with homosexual activism's claims that "hate crimes" are on the rise, which cannot be supported by recent federal hate crime statistics. In this classroom exercise, many of the so-called crimes are actually name-calling incidents, not physical violence. Accordingly, one unit in this curriculum is called "Names Can Really Hurt Us."

Asay. © 1998 by Creators Syndicate, Inc. Reprinted with permission.

This is not to justify hurtful name-calling, but the point is that these curricula stretch the truth in making wildly erroneous connections. It quickly becomes obvious that *speech critical of homosexuality is the target*. The importance of kind and civil behavior toward everyone is a lesson which all parents would support. But by tagging onto genuine civil rights issues, students get the message that homosexuality is harmless and respectable, and furthermore that speech objecting to homosexuality cannot be part of a principled stand in favor of sexual morality, but instead is bigotry leading to violence. The "Healing the Hate" curriculum has been distributed to every school in Massachusetts.

Demonizing Critics

Other curricula like it are available throughout the country. In fact, within one week following the World Trade Center and Pentagon attacks, the developers of "Healing the Hate" unveiled a mini-curriculum called, ironically, "Beyond Blame." Its focus is the unjust treatment of Japanese-Americans and German-Americans during World War II. The recommended resources, however, include material that once again endorses homosexuals as a group, and falsely demonizes Christians and conservatives. PBS has also developed a similar curriculum with the same spurious and intolerant connections.

Religious freedom and freedom of speech issues are threatened by programs like these. Is there to soon be only one acceptable belief system in this country—one that endorses homosexual behavior as 'safe' for even elementary age students? The vast majority of people in this country are not potentially violent and do not deserve to be unjustly associated with violence toward homosexuals!

Now, more than ever before, it's time to stop this unfair stereotyping. . . .

If you read their own material, suppressing freedom of opinion is an expressed goal of GLSEN, and is in fact the essence of the objective to "eradicate homophobia." In their teaching manual called "Tackling Gay Issues in Schools," they state that, "*Every* child, gay and straight alike, is endangered by anti-gay prejudice." One lesson for high school students talks about "oppression" and "oppressors." Some of these oppressors, they tell the students, are heterosexuals, men, Christians, and adults in general.

It's not just vicious brutality and unkindness that are the targets here. GLSEN's material identifies put-downs or derogatory comments as a problem and that "offenders" even in elementary school need to be disciplined. Among the recommendations for these little children are that they meet with an openly gay person or be required to do community service at the local chapter of GLSEN or PFLAG! Another recommendation is to keep lists of students or teachers who commit such infractions.

Advancement of the Gay Agenda

It has been chilling to watch the steady advancement of the "gay" agenda in our schools, and those who are jumping on this bandwagon. Even the mighty National Education Association (NEA) has issued guidelines for schools that include tolerance on the basis of sexual orientation to be part of school safety programs.

Will the NEA come to the defense of a teacher the thought police puts on a list if he or she happens to say something disapproving of homosexuality? The freedom of speech of teachers is just as threatened as that of parents and students.

Just so we are clear about what is considered offensive, let's look at what happened in Naples, Florida recently. The Collier County School Board was considering expanding its anti-harassment policy to name sexual orientation specifically. One parent asked what would be considered "harassment." What about, for instance, the expressed belief that homosexuality is morally wrong? The parent was told by school officials that quite possibly such a viewpoint *would qualify as harassment.*

In looking around for other activities funded by the federal Safe and Drug Free Schools program, we found a very interesting example being implemented in the states of Maine and West Virginia. It's called the Civil Rights Team Project, and operates out of the attorney general's offices in those states. Officials go out to middle schools and train students about harassment and intolerance, including how to identify racist and "homophobic" remarks. These students then are to contact the attorney general's office if they hear homophobic "slurs" from other students. . . .

Are these the ideals for a new concept of childhood? Is this "safety," and part of a new notion of "tolerance"? Not in my view, nor the view, I would suspect, of most of America. If we really want our children to be safe, we will stop this Trojan Horse at the schoolyard gates.

"In 1998, . . . sexual orientation represented the third-highest category of all hate crime victims."

Hate Crime Laws Are Needed to Protect Gays and Lesbians

Elizabeth Birch

In the following viewpoint Elizabeth Birch argues in favor of the Hate Crime Prevention Act (HCPA), a bill that would include sexual orientation in hate crime legislation and provide federal assistance to local law enforcement in the event of a hate crime. The HCPA is necessary, she contends, because hate crimes against homosexuals are increasingly brutal. In Birch's opinion federal legislation that stigmatizes antigay hate crimes could reduce the incidence of future attacks on homosexuals. The HCPA is currently being reviewed by a House committee. Birch is the executive director of the Human Rights Campaign, the nation's largest gay and lesbian political organization.

As you read, consider the following questions:
1. According to the author, why did Congress pass the Church Arson Protection Act in 1996?
2. What is the biggest fallacy perpetrated by opponents to the HCPA, as stated by Birch?
3. According to the author, how could the HCPA have been useful in the Matthew Shepard case?

Elizabeth Birch, "Q: Should Hate Crime Laws Explicitly Protect Sexual Orientation? Yes: Crimes Against Gays and Lesbians Are Widespread and Need Special Treatment," *Insight on the News*, vol. 16, July 24, 2000, pp. 40, 42–43. Copyright © 2000 by News World Communications, Inc. Reproduced by permission.

Although they never met each other and lived more than 1,000 miles apart, University of Wyoming student Matthew Shepard and Alabama textile worker Billy Jack Gaither had one ritual in common. On weekends, they both often would drive several hours to find refuge in big-city gay bars to escape momentarily the stifling, antigay attitudes in the small towns where they resided. Like many gay and lesbian Americans, Shepard and Gaither took these long treks because they understood the potentially dangerous ramifications of getting identified as gay in places where the label makes one a target for violence. Sadly, their suspicions proved to be correct, as they both were murdered in grisly fashion when they failed to take their true identities out of town.

Out of the Shadows

Across America more gay and lesbian people are refusing to live their lives in the shadows. But the increased honesty and visibility that has led to more fulfilling and productive lives for millions of people has been accompanied by a backlash. Most striking about hate crimes is the ferocity and ruthlessness involved in the assaults. A survey by the National Coalition of Anti-Violence Programs reports that in antigay hate crimes in 1998, guns used during assaults grew 71 percent; ropes and restraints, 133 percent; vehicles, 150 percent; and blunt objects, clubs and bats, 47 percent.

These alarming statistics show that the intent of perpetrators is not simply to kill their victims, but to destroy and punish what their victims represent. In a sense, the victims are not the real targets but convenient outlets for those who hate and wish to unleash their bigoted rage and fury against an entire group. In a multicultural country such as America, hate crimes are a form of domestic terrorism and threaten the very fabric of our nation. These crimes are unique in the way they divide society and serve as atomic bombs to national unity. The Hate Crimes Prevention Act, or HCPA, which passed by the Senate 57–42 on June 20, [2000,] is a common-sense measure to address these crimes which have a corrosive effect on society. Unfortunately, extreme groups that oppose its passage in the House are waging an orchestrated campaign of misinformation.

Opponents to hate-crime legislation argue that HCPA is not needed because current laws already exist to punish those who commit hate crimes. But Congress has before recognized that crimes motivated by hate have broad social implications and therefore need to be treated differently. In 1996, Congress passed the Church Arson Protection Act in response to a national outbreak of church burnings. Arson laws already were on the books, but legislators recognized a difference between targeting a church to send a message to parishioners and randomly torching a 7-Eleven. If members of Congress can recognize that the desecration of buildings can be used to intimidate entire communities, they ought to be just as vigilant when the symbol chosen to send a hateful message to a community is a person.

Furthermore, if these opponents truly believed their own rhetoric about "all crimes being hate crimes," they would try in earnest to repeal the existing federal hate-crime law that covers race, religion, color and national origin. But it is clear their only interest lies in making sure sexual orientation isn't covered. Unfortunately, this sends a message that the lives of gay men and women are worth less than those who already are covered. This attitude is inexplicable considering that in 1998 . . . sexual orientation represented the third-highest category of all hate crime victims (16 percent), behind race (56 percent), and religion (18 percent).

"Moral" Objections

Some people have "moral" objections to sexual orientation being added to federal hate-crime laws. HCPA cosponsor Senator Gordon Smith, an Oregon Republican, astutely countered this argument in a 2000 *Washington Post* op-ed. According to Smith, "I often have told those who attempt to wield the sword of morality against others that if they want to talk about sin, go with me to church, but if they want to talk about policy, go with me to the Senate. That is the separation of church and state."

Perhaps the biggest fallacy perpetuated by those on the extreme right is that the HCPA treats some victims more equally than others. The truth is, all people are covered under this inclusive legislation. Those who misleadingly say that this legislation elevates some victims over others must somehow be under the impression that they do not belong to a race, have a religion or a sexual orientation. They can rest easy that if they do, they too will be covered.

Opponents of hate-crime legislation like to obfuscate the issue by saying that hate-crime laws punish thought. However, the HCPA does not apply to hateful thoughts, just violent actions that cause bodily injuries or death. [In 1999], at a recent Senate Judiciary Committee hearing on hate crimes, Judy Shepard, Matthew's mother, best articulated why this argument is false. According to Shepard, "I can assure opponents of this legislation firsthand, it was not words or thoughts, but violent actions that killed my son."

Interestingly, in the 22 states that have hate-crime laws that include sexual orientation, all the dire predictions of the far right have not come to pass. The world has not ended and thoughts or free speech have not been limited.

In fact, the Supreme Court squarely addressed the constitutionality of hate-crime laws in the early 1990s in two cases: *R.A.V. v. City of St. Paul* and *Wisconsin v. Mitchell*. These cases clearly demonstrate that a hate-crime statute may consider bias motivation when that motivation is directly connected to a defendant's criminal conduct. By requiring this connection to criminal activity, these statutes do not chill protected speech and do not violate the First Amendment. In *Wisconsin v. Mitchell*, the Supreme Court made clear that "the First Amendment . . . does not prohibit the evidentiary use of speech to establish the elements of a crime or to prove motive or intent." The HCPA actually would promote free speech by protecting entire groups from being silenced through fear and threats of violence. The right to free speech belongs to all Americans, not just to those who wish to spread hate.

Bringing in the Feds

The focus by some critics on penalties intentionally misses the point of this legislation. The HCPA does not increase penalties for hate crimes. Its purpose is to help law enforcement by allowing federal assistance, when necessary, in the investigation and prosecution of hate crimes. It would do this by providing them with the latest in technical and forensic technology. It also could provide grants of as much as $100,000 to state, local and American Indian law-enforcement officials who have incurred extraordinary expenses associated with investigating and prosecuting hate crimes.

Undermining Equality

The brutal murder [in October 1998] of Matthew Shepard—the twenty-one-year-old gay college student in Wyoming who was beaten and tied to a cross-like fence to die—struck at the conscience of the nation. It was not only the sheer sadism and rancor of the crime that affected Americans, but the sense that Shepard's rights had been violated simply for being who he was.

Hate-motivated crimes have their own pedigree, their own smell. They are acts of criminal violence—among them kidnapping, torture, and murder—but their destructive capacity stems from a motivational intensity that sets them apart. When James Byrd, Jr., a disabled African-American, was dragged to his death in Jasper, Texas, [in] June [1998], every reflective American knew instinctively that this crime was motivated by a particular loathing born of prejudice.

Crimes of this sort can be triggered by a victim's demeanor, color, status, ethnicity, speech, etc., which become the pretext for unleashing blind fury. For potential victims, the threat of such violence is a constant source of vulnerability, unease, fear, even terror. These violent acts of bigotry demand forceful and consistent redress, for they strike at the heart of the solidarity that binds society together; they undermine the very notion of equality.

Patrick Jordan, *Commonweal*, November 20, 1998.

A perfect example of where the HCPA could have been useful was in the Matthew Shepard case. During the investigation, the Albany County [Wyoming] Sheriff's office had to furlough five investigators because of soaring costs. If HCPA were passed, this never would have happened. According to Commander David O'Malley of the Laramie, Wyoming, Police Department, who worked on the investigation, "I call on Congress to give local law-enforcement agencies the tools they need properly to investigate and prosecute hate crimes."

HCPA has broad support from notable law-enforcement

agencies and state and local leaders—including 22 state attorneys general, the National Sheriffs Association, the Police Foundation, the International Association of Chiefs of Police and the U.S. Conference of Mayors.

Opponents who say passing hate-crime legislation will unnecessarily federalize crime not only miss the point that it is supported by law enforcement but that this measure has a precedent. The federal government historically has played a significant role in the prosecution and punishment of civil-rights violations. Although criminal law is traditionally the domain of the states, Congress regularly has criminalized behavior in areas with broad national implications, including organized crime, terrorism, corporate fraud transcending state lines and civil rights. In fact, the federal government has enacted more than 3,000 criminal statutes since 1866—a great many of which have concerned civil rights.

Indeed, while arguing that criminal law is solely an area of state interest, the Republican-controlled Congress has enacted at least 14 laws that create new federal crimes or impose new federal criminal penalties for conduct that is or may also be criminal under state law. These laws address a broad range of issues—from punishing "deadbeat dads" to protecting veterans' cemeteries.

The Right's True Colors

The most insidious argument from those on the extreme right is that gay advocates are using these laws to "legitimize" gay rights. Ironically, these opponents are the only people talking about homosexuality in this debate. They are so obsessed with gay people that they are willing to buck the wishes of law enforcement and deny them the tools they need to solve crimes. They inexplicably believe that in order for their families to succeed and prosper, they must deny justice to the families of hate-crime victims. Fortunately, in their zeal to attack gay people and their families, the true colors of the extreme right have come into clear focus and this is why most Americans support federal crime legislation.

Gay and lesbian Americans who live in hostile environments don't need to see the latest statistics to know that hate crimes are an ever-present threat. In news reports, it was estimated that nearly 100 gay people live in Sylacauga, Alabama, the town of 13,000 where Gaither grew up and was killed. Not one of them is openly gay. Like Gaither and Shepard, these people clearly understand the deadly consequences they may face if their neighbors discover their sexual orientation. Members of Congress should recognize that this palpable climate of fear may exist in their districts. A vote for the Hate Crimes Prevention Act is a vote to correct this grave injustice and protect all citizens fairly and equally.[1]

1. The HCPA is currently being reviewed by a House committee.

"There is no evidence that [hate crime laws] actually prevent hate crimes."

Hate Crime Laws Would Be Ineffective at Protecting Homosexuals

Richard Kim

Richard Kim is the assistant director of the Nation Institute, an organization dedicated to preserving free speech and an independent press. In the following viewpoint he contends that the Hate Crime Prevention Act (HCPA), which would include sexual orientation in hate crime legislation and provide federal resources to local law enforcement in the event of a hate crime, would not reduce the incidence of violence against homosexuals. He argues that laws cannot protect homosexuals from hate crimes, as a significant number of acts of antigay violence are perpetrated by law-enforcement officials themselves. He maintains that community efforts, such as educational workshops in public schools and police academies, would be more effective at combating antigay hate crimes than enacting hate crime legislation. A version of the HCPA was approved by the Senate in 2000 and is currently being reviewed by a House committee.

As you read, consider the following questions:
1. Why does the author believe that passing the HCPA would be mainly symbolic?
2. What did the National Coalition of Antiviolence Programs discover about antigay harassment by police in their 1998 report, as cited by the author?

Richard Kim, "The Truth About Hate Crime Laws," *Nation*, vol. 26, July 12, 1999, p. 20. Copyright © 1999 by The Nation Magazine/The Nation Company, Inc. Reproduced by permission.

For whatever reasons, it took the death of a young gay white man at the hands of two other young white men in Wyoming to bring the issue of violence aimed at lesbians, gays, bisexuals and transgendered people (LGBT) to national consciousness. While one of those young men, Russell Henderson, has pleaded guilty to murder, kidnapping and robbery, and while another, Aaron McKinney, awaits trial, national lesbian and gay organizations have focused the fear, anger, compassion and political capital aroused by Matthew Shepard's killing into a campaign for federal and state hate crimes legislation. [Henderson and McKinney were convicted of felony murder and each sentenced to two consecutive life terms in 1999.]

All Together Now

The Gay and Lesbian Alliance Against Defamation, the Human Rights Campaign (HRC), the National Gay and Lesbian Task Force (NGLTF), and Parents, Families and Friends of Lesbians And Gays, along with an assortment of religious ethnic-feminist and civil rights groups, have all pursued hate crimes legislation. They are joined by [former] President Clinton, most Congressional Democrats and even a few Republicans, such as Senator Arlen Specter, who have endorsed the federal Hate Crimes Prevention Act (HCPA), a version of which failed to pass 1998's Congress despite having more than 200 co-sponsors and some bipartisan support.

Hate crimes legislation denotes a set of prescriptions that include toughening sentencing guidelines, expanding federal jurisdiction and requiring the compilation of statistical data on bias crimes. (On the federal level, the Hate Crimes Statistics Act, passed in 1990, already requires the FBI to collect data on anti-LGBT violence.) Currently, twenty-one states and the District of Columbia have hate crimes laws with provisions on sexual orientation along with race, religion, ethnicity and, in some cases, disability and gender; twenty states have hate crimes laws that do not include sexual orientation, and nine states have no hate crimes laws whatsoever.

Even as national lesbian and gay organizations pursue hate crimes laws with single-minded fervor, concentrating precious resources and energy on these campaigns, there is no evidence that such laws actually prevent hate crimes. Passage of the federal HCPA would be largely symbolic: Although it would expand the potential for federal prosecution of anti-LGBT bias crimes, for the most part it would allow legislators to appear to be doing something about homophobia without actually addressing its cultural roots. Meanwhile, beneath the national radar, local antiviolence projects focused on community organizing, outreach and education—efforts that attempt to stop gay-bashing by changing the social environment in which it occurs—are struggling with scant resources.

Dubious Law Enforcement

HRC and other national gay and lesbian organizations contend that if hate crimes laws are passed, law enforcement officials will not only report anti-LGBT violence but will also have the mandate and resources to prosecute it. Yet HRC's political director, Winnie Stachelberg, concedes that "local law enforcement agencies are often reluctant to report [such] crimes," and there is little reason to think that such reluctance would dissolve in the face of a new law. A 1998 report by the National Coalition of Anti-Violence Programs, a network of community-based organizations that monitor and respond to anti-LGBT violence, notes that instances of verbal harassment and abuse by police officers increased by 155 percent from 1997 to 1998, and reports of physical abuse by police grew by more than 866 percent. Given that law enforcement officials regularly harass gays and lesbians—and that antisodomy laws that enable such behavior are still on the books in eighteen states—it seems improbable that passage of hate crimes laws would suddenly transform the state into a guardian of gay and lesbian people.

Community antiviolence activists are intimately aware of this reality. In San Francisco, for example, Shawna Virago, a male-to-female transsexual activist with Community United Against Violence (CUAV), reports that law enforcement officials are not only indifferent to anti-LGBT violence but are often perpetrators of such acts. In 1998, she notes, 50 percent of reported incidents of violence against transgendered people in the Bay Area were committed by law enforcement

Disapproval of Homosexuality Is Not a Crime

It is generally wrong to disapprove of people because of their religion, race, or gender, but it is not a crime. (An exception may be disapproval of someone whose religion includes committing terrorist acts.) The purpose of the gay movement and its advocates . . . is to criminalize disapproval of homosexual acts, or at least to establish in law that such disapproval is disapproved. Most Americans, it may safely be assumed, disapprove of homosexual acts. It is not within the competence of the state to declare that they are, for that reason, legally suspect. In a sinful world, sundry hatreds, irrational prejudices, and unjust discriminations abound. The homosexual movement is notable for its venting of hatred against millions of Americans whom it accuses of being "homophobic." In whatever form it takes, hatred toward other people must be deplored and condemned. But it is utterly wrongheaded to try to make hatred illegal.

Richard John Newhans, *First Things*, January 1999.

officials. CUAV works alongside other antiviolence campaigns, such as the Bay Area Police Watch, youth groups and minority organizations, to compile its own statistical data on bias crimes; conduct educational workshops in public schools, social service agencies and police academies; create safer public spaces; and combat illegal strip searches of transgendered people by police officers. Given the pervasive homophobia of law enforcement agencies, these measures seem far better suited to the task of stemming anti-LGBT violence than hate crimes legislation.

Lengthening Prison Sentences

In seeking federal prosecution and increased penalties for hate crimes, the NGLTF has argued that "criminal activity based on prejudice terrorizes not only victims but the entire community of which they are a part," and the HRC has said that "hate crimes affect more than just the individual attacked. . . . Hate crimes rend the fabric of society and fragment communities." Undoubtedly, lesbian, gay, bisexual and transgendered communities suffer fear and intimidation from violent assaults, but hate crimes laws are aimed at lengthening prison sentences, not creating safer community spaces.

Aaron McKinney and Russell Henderson, for instance,

attacked Matthew Shepard at least in part to rob him, and McKinney attacked two Hispanic youths shortly after leaving Shepard for dead—making it clear that Shepard's murder occurred in the context of hostile racial and class relations, which hate crimes legislation would do nothing to address. In gentrifying or gentrified urban areas, such as New York's West Village, Chelsea and Park Slope, anti-LGBT violence occurs as existing populations are displaced by waves of lesbian and gay migration. Again, hate crimes legislation fails to grapple with this community problem.

Investing in local organizing, on the other hand, not only enables activists to connect the struggle against anti-gay and lesbian violence to such issues as job protection and the repeal of sodomy laws, it also builds gay and lesbian communities and creates safer social spaces—while at the same time reaching out to other communities to combat the problem of violence together. That's something no hate crimes law will ever do.[1]

1. The HCPA is currently being reviewed by a House committee.

"Whatever fancy words [moralists] dress themselves in, they really are inciters of hate against gays and lesbians."

Criticism of Homosexuality Leads to Violence Toward Gays and Lesbians

Anonymous

In the following viewpoint an anonymous contributor to the *National Catholic Reporter* argues that members of the religious right speak about homosexuality with blatant hostility. These people who vilify homosexuals, according to the author, are influential leaders of popular conservative organizations, such as the Christian Coalition and Focus on the Family. Their hate-filled rhetoric, the author contends, incites some people to commit violence toward gays and lesbians.

As you read, consider the following questions:

1. According to the author, how has the Catholic Church contributed to an atmosphere of hatred toward homosexuals?
2. What was the basis of the Family Research Council's ad campaign, in the author's opinion?
3. How does John Eldredge perceive the "gay agenda," as quoted by the author?

Anonymous, "Pious Veneer Can't Hide Hate," *National Catholic Reporter*, vol. 35, October 23, 1998, p. 28. Copyright © 1998 by National Catholic Reporter, www.natcath.org. Reproduced by permission.

In May 1994 anti-gay activists of the Christian right from around the country gathered in secret session in Colorado Springs, Colorado, to discuss a strategy for reversing political gains made by the gay rights movement.

Thinking they were out of earshot of the media, their speech was often informal and unguarded. They had planned it that way so they could say what they wished without being held accountable by a wider public.

But their comments were captured on tape recordings that were passed on to the *National Catholic Reporter* (NCR), which published a story based on the tapes in its September 2, 1994, issue. What came out of that gathering was an ugly, hate-filled stripping away of humanity from those who are homosexual, vilifying any who would seek protection under law from discrimination because of sexual orientation.

Tracing Hateful Thoughts

It might be inaccurate to draw a straight line from that gathering in Colorado to the site in Laramie, Wyoming, where in 1998 Matthew Shepard was lashed to a fence, tortured and beaten because he was gay. Shepard, a 21-year-old college student, died as a result of the beating.

It is absolutely essential, however, that we trace the thought that motivated that meeting—as well as all the accumulated, hate-filled blather from the "religious" right, fundamentalist Catholic and Protestant alike—and follow it as it winds its way to that killing place in Wyoming.

Sadly, the Catholic church, having given gay-bashers the incredible phrase that homosexuality itself "must be seen as an objective disorder" cannot be spared some blame for contributing to the atmosphere that inspires hate. To their credit, however, the U.S. bishops generally have not joined the extremists and have gone against the prevailing tide in U.S. culture, as well as in Rome, with the release of [a] compassionate pastoral letter, "Always Our Children." And there are other examples, such as that of Archbishop William Levada of San Francisco . . . who was able to work a compromise with city government over a gay partners' law.

But the groups that constitute the religious right have shown no such balance. [In the summer of 1998,] Gary Bauer's

Family Research Council was behind a hideous ad campaign displaying alleged former homosexuals who claim that through religious conversion they had become heterosexual.

His group and others [followed] up with a new battery of ads aimed clearly at achieving political gain by demonizing homosexuals. Of course, it is not that blatant. These tacticians are shameless enough to end their ads with the slogan: "It's not about hate. . . . It's about hope."

In the Social Interest

Rules against hate speech, homophobic remarks and misogyny serve both symbolic and institutional values—increasing productivity in the workplace and protecting a learning environment on campus. It has been argued that such prohibitions operate in derogation of the First Amendment's guarantee of freedom of speech, but that amendment already is subject to dozens of exceptions—libel, defamation, words of conspiracy or threat, disrespectful words uttered to a judge or police officer, irrelevant or untrue words spoken in a judicial proceeding, copyright, plagiarism, official secrets, misleading advertising and many more. The social interest in deterring vicious racial or sexual vituperation certainly seems at least as great as that underlying these other forms of speech deemed unworthy of First Amendment protection.

Richard Delgado, *Insight on the News*, June 24, 1996.

But it is about hate. Catch the unguarded conversation [in 1994] of Paul Cameron, who identified himself as a psychologist and chairman of the Family Research Institute. He was talking about someone in Canada who had a message on his home phone recorder "about what ought to be done with queers."

The same Family Research Council was spitting out press releases denouncing the Shepard killing [in 1998], but also expressing concern "that some members of the media and representatives of homosexual organizations may be fueling hostility toward Christians and people of other faiths who believe homosexuality is morally objectionable. . . . Our message is about offering homosexuals the choice to change."

That's what they and their ilk would like the public to believe. Whatever fancy words they dress themselves in, they really are inciters of hate against gays and lesbians.

Take the unguarded words of John Eldredge, a leader of James Dobson's influential Focus on the Family, which also spews its venom while draped in religious costume. At that secret meeting, Eldredge said: "I think the gay agenda—I would not say this as frankly as I will now in other cultural contexts—I think the gay agenda has all the elements of that which is truly evil." This is a so-called religious leader speaking. He could scarcely find more explicit words to give permission to his followers to go out and stomp out that "evil."

Eldredge was joined, of course, by representatives of Pat Robertson and his Christian Coalition, one of the most successful religious charades of modern times.

It was clear in that secret session in Colorado that the god of the gay-bashers is a menacing and vindictive god, one who joins in jeering those who are different, in condemning those on the margin, who mocks the humanity of those who, through no fault or choice of their own, have a sexual orientation that is different from that of the majority.

That is the god behind the ads and the sanctimonious campaigns to demonize gays and lesbians.

It is a god for whom the Christian scriptures would have to be rewritten—and it is a god who should be soundly rejected.

If Bauer and other evangelists of this god are feeling the heat, it's about time.

"It apparently no longer is acceptable to hold differing views on the rightness of homosexuality."

Criticism of Homosexuality Is Not Wrong

Steven Greenhut

According to *Lima News* editor Steven Greenhut, anyone who expresses disapproval of homosexuality is automatically labeled a bigot in today's society. He argues that many Americans believe that homosexuality is wrong, and they should not be afraid to express their views. He maintains that honest discussion of important issues requires that all opinions be given a voice. *Lima News* is a newspaper from Lima, Ohio.

As you read, consider the following questions:

1. In the author's opinion, what is the original meaning of tolerance?
2. What does Trent Lott compare homosexuality to, as quoted by Greenhut?
3. According to the author, how has America strayed too far from its founding principles?

Given the state of current discourse, in which honest observations that conflict with the zeitgeist are zealously punished, I begin my column with this caveat: I harbor no hatred against homosexuals, am offended by anti-gay discrimination, in no way condone violence against them and really couldn't care less what sexual behavior adults engage in.

I thought of this admittedly wimpy approach after following what Senate Majority Leader Trent Lott had to go through [in 1998] for making some seemingly innocuous comments about homosexuality on a TV talk show. You never know how left-wingers will misconstrue what you say, so it's important to pre-empt the predictable hysteria.

Unacceptable Views

Of course, my caveat probably won't help me with the thought police because I subscribe to some unacceptable views: I believe homosexuality is wrong. I suspect that even if homosexual tendencies are biologically predetermined, choice is involved in "becoming" gay. And I am convinced most of the gay-rights agenda is an attack on freedom and property rights because it would use government power to squelch dissent and promote "civil rights."

It used to be OK to say such things and to stand up for tolerance in its original sense: Putting up with—though not endorsing—behavior you find offensive or immoral.

But not any more.

It's not as if Lott made derogatory comments about gays or proposed laws that would relegate gays and lesbians to the margins of society. He said homosexuality is a sin—a theological position held by most religions and probably by most Americans—and that we should be willing to help gays overcome what Lott terms a "problem."

You needn't agree with that assessment to realize that Lott perpetrated no hate crime, that his view is not out of the American mainstream, and that it is no more moralistic than the quasi-theological pronouncements [former] Vice President Al Gore and Interior Secretary Bruce Babbitt regularly make about the sanctity of Mother Earth and the godliness of the multicultural agenda.

Here's what happened:

After TV host Armstrong Williams asked Lott whether he viewed homosexuality as a sin, Lott said it is, then remarked: "You should still love that person. You should not try to mistreat them or treat them as outcasts. You should try to show them a way to deal with that problem, just like alcohol . . . or sex addiction . . . or kleptomaniacs. There are all kinds of problems, addictions, difficulties, experiences of things that are wrong, but you should try to work with that person to learn to control that problem." Is that so awful?

A Media Frenzy

Yet these gentle words sparked a media frenzy, with the TV networks devoting far more airtime to the controversy than to the president's possible trading of advanced missile technology to China for campaign cash, or to any other legitimate news story.

Most hilarious was this response from Mike McCurry, the White House flack whose shameless defense of [former President Bill Clinton's] many misdeeds should preclude him from making unctuous pronouncements about any moral issue:

> For over 25 years, it's been quite clear that sexual orientation is not an affliction, it is not a disease, it is something that is a part of defining one's sexuality. And the fact that the majority leader has such views, apparently consistent with some who are fairly extreme in his party, is an indicator of how difficult it is to do rational work in Washington.

I'm no fan of the religious right. And I would be outraged if Lott had proposed to use government to reform or oppress homosexuals. But don't believe the gay rights propagandists: No respectable politician (an oxymoron?) of any party would propose anything of the sort these days.

What's happening here is a no-holds-barred attempt at thought control. It apparently no longer is acceptable to hold differing views on the rightness of homosexuality, let alone express them even in the most obsequious and well-intentioned manner.

To the administration and other gay-rights zealots, it simply is undemocratic to suggest that homosexuality is wrong, and the worst sort of extremism to oppose government attempts to mandate spousal benefits for gay partners and promulgate anti-discrimination laws that whittle away at the declining number of property rights Americans still enjoy.

A Dainty Sensibility

To the detriment of the homosexual community, the simple act of disapproval with the homosexual lifestyle has become "hate speech." According to the hopelessly irrational logic of the homosexual rights crowd, here are the typical "hate" lines: "Homosexuality is a sin against God," "Homosexuals don't have to act on their sexual desires," and "Homosexuality is a choice and homosexuals can leave the lifestyle behind and convert to heterosexuality."

It is indeed a dainty sensitivity that deems those lines hate speech. Imagine the shocked hysteria if one blurted out a "hate filled" opinion like, "White shoes shouldn't be worn after Labor Day."

Unfortunately, at the utterance of any variation of these "offensive" lines, every homosexual group begins covering their ears and shouting "Hate monger!" Following the illogic, another vicious hate monger line is: "Ax murder is a sin against God." To be consistent, the homosexual political action groups should ask Alcoholics Anonymous to bar "hate language" like "alcoholics have a choice about whether to take a drink or not" from their AA meetings. [editor's note: Senate Majority Leader Trent Lott, football legend and minister Reggie White and others are accused of "hate speech" when they list homosexuality among the standard list of human sins.] Thus, there is no room for dialogue or debate with homosexual activists because the holding of a contrary opinion is defined as hate.

D. Marty Lasley, *American Wasteland*, November 1999.

The overheated media response was indicative of the totalitarian way liberal elites intimidate into silence those who disagree with them. I'm sure most Americans got the message: Criticize homosexuality at your own peril. You may be turned into an outcast, called a religious fanatic or face a harassment lawsuit if you express your views to the wrong person.

Believing in Religious Tenets

A similar spectacle took place [in 1998] when the Southern Baptists dared to suggest the family is sacrosanct. They also said wives should submit graciously to husbands. As all Baptists surely know, the submission part is followed in Scripture by Christ's admonition for men to sacrifice themselves to their wives, as Christ sacrificed himself for the church—not nearly as unfair a situation as network news shows portrayed it to be.

What's really intolerable, of course, is that a religious denomination actually believes in the tenets of its faith. It would be far more acceptable to modern liberals had the Baptists done what many mainline congregations and theologians do: abandon time-tested principles in favor of gay rights, feminism, abortion rights and other fixations of progressive minds.

People often ask, "How did America move so far away from its founding principles of liberty, and from the values that have made that liberty possible?" The answer, in part, is through concerted intimidation campaigns against "incorrect" views by those on the liberal cutting edge.

You needn't be a foe of gay rights or a proponent of traditional marriage to realize that honest discussions of political and moral issues should not be confined to the limited parameters established by modern-day Torquemadas.[1] Right or wrong, Lott's words are hardly a hanging offense, and the more of us who say so, the quicker the national media will move on to other subjects.

---

1. Tomás de Torquemadas was the grand inquisitor of the Spanish Inquisition in 1478. Under his authority, thousands of Jews, suspected witches, and others were killed or tortured.

Periodical Bibliography

The following articles have been selected to supplement the diverse views presented in this chapter.

Carlos A. Ball — "That We Are Human, We Have Rights," *Gay & Lesbian Review Worldwide*, November/December 2002.

Chris Bull and Judy Wieder — "Scene of the Crime; Laws Against Gay Sex Can Block Everything We Want: Marriage, Adoption, and Equal Rights," *Advocate*, October 27, 1998.

Deborah Dallinger — "We Just Want to Be Ourselves," *San Francisco Chronicle*, June 25, 1998.

Chai R. Feldblum — "Moral Law, Changing Morals," *Nation*, October 9, 2000.

Wesley Granberg-Michaelson — "Many Members, One Body," *Sojourners*, May 1999.

William Norman Grigg — "Why Should We Care?" *New American*, November 18, 2002.

Thomas J. Gumbleton — "Yes, Gay Men Should Be Ordained," *America*, September 30, 2002.

Justin Raimondo — "A Gay Man Decries 'Gay Rights,'" *American Enterprise*, March 2000.

Jonathan Rauch — "The Last Gasp of Jim Crow," *National Journal*, November 21, 1998.

Richard Rohr — "Where the Gospel Leads Us," *Other Side*, September 1999.

Gabriel Rotello — "Gay and Lesbian Rights," *Social Policy*, Spring 1998.

Jody Veenker — "Called to Hate?" *Christianity Today*, October 25, 1999.

Robert Weissberg — "The Abduction of Tolerance," *Society*, November/December 1998.

Mickey Wheatley — "On Being Homosexual in the 21st Century," *Social Policy*, Summer 2000.

Riki Wilchins — "Because That's What We Do to Faggots," *Advocate*, October 21, 2001.

CHAPTER 3

Is Homosexuality Immoral?

Chapter Preface

Since the dawn of the gay rights movement in the late 1960s, religious leaders have cited passages from the Bible that they say support their belief that homosexuality is immoral and sinful. The church's position on homosexuality quickly caused a rift between staunch believers and gays and lesbians who resented being told that they were evil and depraved. Recently, several gay and lesbian activists examined the biblical passages in question and interpreted them as indifferent to homosexuality. Biblical scholars and homosexual advocates are now deeply divided over whether the Bible condemns homosexuality.

Religious leaders typically cite seven passages from the Bible that they allege condemn homosexuality. One of the most frequently cited passages, found in Genesis 19, is the story of the destruction of Sodom. The story is so frequently used to condemn homosexuality that the term "sodomite," which once referred to an inhabitant of the city of Sodom, became a legal term for criminal sexual acts and is now used as a derogatory synonym for a homosexual. Genesis 19 describes how two angels visited the city of Sodom and were welcomed as guests into the home of an elderly citizen named Lot. A group of men approached Lot's house and demanded that he bring the strangers out to the mob so that they might "know" them. Lot refused and offered his two virgin daughters to the mob in lieu of the angels. The offer was declined, a fight ensued, and God ultimately destroyed the city of Sodom, sparing Lot and his daughters.

Conservative Christians interpret the story of the destruction of Sodom as an unequivocal condemnation of homosexual acts. They argue that the word "know" in this context means to know someone sexually. Thus, conservatives contend that in "knowing" the angels means that the mob wished to engage in anal intercourse with the angels. The fact that Lot offers his daughters to the mob instead of the angels, according to conservative interpretations, reveals that the mob's intention was purely sexual. Moreover, offering his daughters to the mob as a sexual replacement for the angels clearly implies that heterosexual rape of virgins is less abominable in the eyes of God than homosexual rape, according to some interpretations. Conservatives maintain that the men of Sodom were uninterested in Lot's daughters because the men were homosexual. God destroyed the city, some people argue, because he was angry with the citizens for engaging in homosexual acts. As stated by R. Albert Mohler, president of the Southern Baptist Theological Seminary, "The Genesis passage is very clear, that the sin of Sodom that brought on the destruction of the city was indeed linked to homosexuality."

Gay and lesbian activists and their supporters maintain that such interpretations of the destruction of Sodom take the story out of its proper context. They argue that the sin of Sodom was inhospitality, not homosexuality. These experts contend that Sodom was surrounded by harsh geographical conditions, so a cardinal rule in Lot's society was to offer hospitality to travelers. Lot graciously welcomed the angels into his home, but the other citizens of Sodom attempted to attack and rape the angels. Experts contend that when the story was written, men commonly raped captured soldiers or prisoners to shame and humiliate their enemies. Thus, the attempted rape of the angels was driven by violence and inhospitality, not homosexual desires. Homosexual advocates argue that this interpretation explains why the men refused Lot's daughters; the men were not seeking sexual gratification. God destroyed Sodom, these analysts contend, because he was angry that its citizens were inhospitable to the visiting angels. As stated by author Ronda DeVold, "Abuse and offense against strangers, insult to the traveler, inhospitality to the needy, and sexual abuse. That is the point of the story understood in its historical context."

The destruction of Sodom is just one Bible passage used to justify antipathy toward homosexuals and their lifestyle. Conservative Christians argue that there are several more passages that unequivocally state that homosexuality is wrong in the eyes of God. However, other Bible scholars interpret the same passages as indifferent to homosexuality. The authors in the following chapter discusses different interpretations of the Bible's position on homosexuality, among other issues.

"Homosexuals themselves understand their behavior is immoral."

Homosexual Behavior Is Immoral

Tom Ambrose

According to Tom Ambrose in the following viewpoint, homosexual behavior is morally wrong. He argues that homosexuals engage in irresponsible sexual practices that God has declared sinful. Moreover, he maintains, gays and lesbians flaunt their behavior rather than repent of it. Ambrose is the commentary editor of *WorldNetDaily*, a conservative online journal.

As you read, consider the following questions:

1. According to the author, what was the leading ethic in the 1970s?
2. Why should homosexual behavior not be considered a civil right, in Ambrose's opinion?
3. How do homosexuals flaunt their behavior, as stated by the author?

Some of you may remember back to the San Francisco riots in the 1970s when the homosexual-rights movement found its voice after members of their community were beaten and murdered. Many, including myself, felt sympathy for what they were going through. At the same time, one particularly vocal opponent of this movement, Anita Bryant, was mocked with signs like, "We don't want your children, Anita, just your husband." She was made to appear as an extremist idiot by the media.

Evil Becomes Morally Acceptable

I was in high school during this turbulent era—a time when Vietnam had closed down and the Watergate hearings had concluded. Other government institutions and politicians were being deservedly exposed for their own corrupt activities. Anti-communism had been equated with McCarthyism. Bizarre religious cults were thriving. And the U.S. Supreme Court had recently allowed uterine-infanticide if the mother chose to do so. Many things that people had generally understood as evil were newly pronounced as morally acceptable. It felt like our nation was being ripped apart. In reality, that was exactly what was happening.

Specifically, biblical values were being trashed in favor of more expedient and self-serving notions. The leading ethic was, "If it feels good, do it." Premarital sex, adultery, homosexuality, pornography, divorce, drug usage—all enjoyed a rapid rise in popularity. Forget the consequences. Forget God. Just do it. And we did.

And we still do.

Since that time, however, the consequences of these activities have also manifested in our nation. Venereal disease, herpes, AIDS, hepatitis, abortion, violence, and crime are destroying America from within. Many of our children are more capable of putting on a condom than they are able to do math or explain why the Constitution is important. We bow to the almighty dollar instead of God.

Anything goes these days.

Even our politicians are but a mere reflection of us because we are the ones who let them get into office either by voting for them or by refusing to vote at all. So, is it any wonder that President George W. Bush is brown-nosing homosexual lobbyists? . . .

Problem Behavior

Look, folks, I do not hate homosexuals, and I am not "homophobic." My maternal grandfather was a closet homosexual. Some of my favorite teachers were homosexual. Some of my friends and neighbors are homosexual. I count these individuals as decent, hardworking, loveable people who either are or were a valued part of my life.

But just because I care for these people does not prevent me from disagreeing with their behavior.

To be sure, homosexual sexual behavior is not any more "irresponsible" than premarital sex or adulterous sexual behavior—the Bible makes it clear that *all* sexual behavior outside of the bounds of heterosexual marriage is sin against God. Nor does the Bible say that homosexuality is a worse sin than other sins. Nor does the Bible teach Christians to be abusive and malicious towards those who sin—including homosexuals—but to love them as Christ has loved us and to invite them to consider following God instead of their path to self-destruction.

At the same time, let's also acknowledge that there is no evidence of a genetic basis for homosexual behavior. Nonetheless, in a society of victimology and dysfunctionality—where it is politically correct to be helpless and hopeless (to the point now where you no longer even are responsible for murdering your children because of your genetic makeup and upbringing)—the homosexual lobby has corruptly seized this mindset as their own.

But, the cry of "we cannot help what we are" implicitly acknowledges that even homosexuals themselves understand their behavior is immoral and that they are not willing to take responsibility for what they do. After all, why do you need to blame genetics for who you are if there is nothing wrong with your behavior?

The Civil Rights Issue

Moreover, homosexual lobbyists have even tried to tie themselves to Martin Luther King's belt buckle by asserting homosexual behavior to be the equivalent of a civil right—a notion repudiated by King's niece—by suggesting that opposition to homosexual behavior is the same thing as racism. Hogwash. People are not responsible for their skin color, but they ought to be responsible for their personal conduct.

Asay. © by Colorado Springs Gazette Telegraph. Reprinted by permission of Creators Syndicate, Inc.

Just as those who are tempted to commit adultery or engage in premarital sex are instructed in Scripture to not act on these primal urges, so too for those who are tempted by homosexual inclinations. There is a way to deal effectively with all of these troubling but illicit desires and that way is provided by God through prayer and forgiveness. For homosexuals seeking freedom from these desires, forgiveness often must be extended to a parent—usually the father—for some real or perceived breach in their relationship with that person from early in their childhood. A breach which they try to repair and restore subconciously by acting out that relationship through homosexual surrogates.

It's about time we got a grip on this issue.

The real problem here is not that homosexuals are sinners

like the rest of us, it is that they flaunt—rather than repent of—what they are doing. They are trying to indoctrinate our children in their way of life through the public schools. They are trying to silence opposition to what they do through legislative bullying and intimidation. They are trying to destroy the long-standing institution of marriage. And they are trying to decimate entire church denominations which do not capitulate to their demands.

In short, they are trying to destroy our way of life—life that was given to us from the time of Adam and Eve, not Adam and Steve. And they are succeeding. Indeed, they have gone way too far. And we have let them.

Fight the Perversion

What homosexuals do in their bedrooms is between them and God. But what they do on our school boards and in our legislatures and churches is all of our business and we had better come to terms with this nasty fact of life soon before we lose our rights—and our children—to this twisted perversion of life.

Vermont has already fallen prey to homosexual activists and malfeasant legislators.[1] And so will go the rest of the nation if we don't stand up to this evil now. Just as Joseph McCarthy has been proven correct about the threats of communism and socialism to our nation, so too have Anita Bryant and many Christian leaders been proven correct about the insidious, debilitating nature of the homosexual-rights movement.

Ultimately, just as the consequences for our immoral behaviors have manifested in destroying our nation, we are also going to have to come to terms with the sovereign God who created us. It's your decision, of course, but I would invite you to consider now whether your relationship with God will be one that is honoring to Him or one of contempt for Him and His ways. But this time, your choice will have *eternal* consequences.

---

1. In 2000 Vermont became the first state to legalize civil unions, which offer homosexual couples the rights and privileges associated with marriage.

"[Homosexuals] should be arguing that our view is better than the anti-gay view—more moral, more reasonable, more humane."

Homosexual Behavior Is Not Immoral

Paul Varnell

In the following viewpoint Paul Varnell contends that most arguments against gay rights rest on the allegation that homosexual behavior is morally wrong. However, according to Varnell, these arguments are irrational because antigay activists fail to explain why homosexual behavior is immoral. Moreover, Varnell maintains that similar arguments against civil rights for women and African Americans were proven immoral and bigoted. Varnell argues that gay rights can only be won when homosexual leaders convince society that homosexual behavior is not immoral. Varnell is a columnist at the *Chicago Free Press* and an editor of the Independent Gay Forum (found at www.indegayforum.org), an online source for discussion of gay-related issues.

As you read, consider the following questions:
1. What problems does moral condemnation of homosexuality generate, according to Varnell?
2. Why does Joseph Lieberman believe that people who disapprove of homosexuality are not bigots?
3. In Varnell's opinion, what is the test for morality?

The fundamental controverted issue about homosexuality is not discrimination, hate crimes or domestic partnerships, but the morality of homosexuality.

Even if gays obtain non-discrimination laws, hate crimes law and domestic partnership benefits, those can do little to counter the underlying moral condemnation which will continue to fester beneath the law and generate hostility, fuel hate crimes, support conversion therapies, encourage gay youth suicide and inhibit the full social acceptance that is our goal.

On the other hand, if we convince people that homosexuality is fully moral then all their inclination to discriminate, engage in gay-bashing or oppose gay marriage disappears. Gay youths and adults could readily accept themselves.

A Moral Revolution

So the gay movement, whether we acknowledge it or not, is not a civil rights movement, not even a sexual liberation movement, but a moral revolution aimed at changing people's view of homosexuality.

In this light, consider a disturbing speech by Senator Joseph Lieberman, D-Conn., [the 2000] Democratic nominee for vice president, printed in the Congressional Record of July 10, 1998. Lieberman said:

> Many Americans continue to believe that homosexuality is immoral and not just because the Bible tells them so. . . .

> This is one of the few areas where Americans of all religious inclinations feel so strongly that they are willing to risk the tag of intolerance to express or hold to their points of view. . . .

> It is unfair, then, for anyone to automatically conclude that people who express moral reservations or even disdain about homosexuality are bigots, or to publicly attack them as hateful. These are sincerely held morally based views.

Lieberman does not quite say he himself regards homosexuality as immoral. He does say that people who think so and express disdain about homosexuality are not bigots.

The reason they are not bigots, Lieberman says, is that their views are sincerely held and morally based. We know that, he says, because they are willing to risk being accused of intolerance in order to express their opinion.

So if you are willing to risk the accusation of intolerance, then we know your view is sincerely held and morally based and you are not a bigot.

Blank Out

Another way we know a view is morally based, Lieberman says, is that although some people hold it because the Bible says so, others hold it because something else—"not just the Bible"—says so.

What is that something else? Lieberman shies away from telling us. It is just . . . something else. As [philosopher and author] Ayn Rand used to say about similar evasions, "Blank Out!"

But making a moral claim, even on behalf of others, does not relieve anyone of the responsibility for explaining its basis. The test for morality is not consensus, or fervor or sincerity, but reason.

Individual Morality

The overwhelming majority of people believe that homosexuality is immoral. I do not. I believe that homosexuality is amoral and that homosexuals individually are either moral or immoral.

Joseph Adam Pearson, *Whosoever*, October 1997.

People disagree about whether many things are moral or immoral. The only way to decide which is right is by examining the reasons people offer.

But people who cannot or will not tell us what reasons support reservations about or disdain for homosexuality are refusing to engage in rational discussion.

And holding strong views without providing defensible reasons is what we usually mean by "bigotry."

Countering Bigotry

There are four counter-arguments we can make.

First is the standard, boilerplate condemnation of so-called hate-speech: "All fair minded Americans and progressive thinking people will surely condemn such harmful and divisive speech," etc., etc.

This kind of talk no doubt makes self-avowed "fair minded and progressive thinking" people feel good about themselves, but it does nothing to convince people who are not already convinced, which you would hope is the main point of making a response at all.

Second is the familiar school yard rebuttal of "Well, that's just your opinion." The adult version is, "We live in a pluralistic society where people hold diverse moral views about these issues." Both versions amount to saying that all opinions are equal so the anti-gay view has no more validity than any other.

But this has the unfortunate corollary that our own pro-gay opinion is no better than the anti-gay one, so there is no reasons for anyone to take our view more seriously than any other. To the contrary, we should be arguing that our view is better than the anti-gay view—more moral, more reasonable, more humane, etc.

Historical Examples of Bigotry

A third response is to remind people of the familiar historical counter-examples where "sincerely held, morally based" views based not only on the Bible were clearly immoral and maybe even bigoted.

Slavery and racial segregation are two obvious examples. Another would be the lengthy resistance to legal and social equality for women. A fourth would be the long, painful history of anti-Semitism, something Senator Lieberman should be well aware of.

But these examples only prove that some sincerely held morally based views are wrong. They do not prove that all such views are wrong—clearly some are not—nor that they are wrong about homosexuality.

In any case, these are merely defensive maneuvers, meant only to neutralize anti-gay views. They do nothing to generate pro-gay views or encourage people to see homosexuality as moral.

So we need a fourth response, offering affirmative reasons for why our sexuality and our sexual behavior are moral. But that means our spokespeople would have to engage in moral reasoning and most seem surprisingly reluctant to do that.

If they cannot or will not, perhaps we need better leaders.

"If the Bible does not teach that sodomy is a sin, it doesn't teach anything is a sin."

The Bible Condemns Homosexuality

D. James Kennedy

In the following viewpoint D. James Kennedy argues that the Bible unequivocally states that homosexual behavior is wrong. He cites passages from Leviticus, Corinthians, and Romans that he claims support the position that God intended people to engage in heterosexual relationships. According to Kennedy, Christians should denounce homosexuality while supporting the efforts of people trying to stop committing homosexual sin. Kennedy is senior minister of Coral Ridge Presbyterian Church in Fort Lauderdale, Florida. He is also chancellor of Knox Theological Seminary in Fort Lauderdale.

As you read, consider the following questions:

1. According to Kennedy, why was the city of Sodom destroyed?
2. Why must Christians avoid hatred, according to the author?
3. What is the difference between "defining deviancy down" and "defining deviancy up," according to Kennedy?

D. James Kennedy, "Leading Voices Under Attack," *Moody*, March/April 1996. Copyright © 1996 by Moody Magazine. Reproduced by permission.

Recently, a leader in the homosexual rights movement asked to see me. Toward the end of our meeting he said one of the most astonishing things I've ever heard on the subject. "The Bible nowhere even mentions homosexuality," he stated. Unfortunately, our time was over and I couldn't discuss with him what the Scriptures do say. Today the "gay lifestyle" has grabbed a lot of attention, and many people twist the Scriptures to justify the sin.

God's Word, however, is clear:

"If a man lies with a man as one lies with a woman, both of them have done what is detestable" (Lev. 20:13).

"God gave them over to shameful lusts. Even their women exchanged natural relations for unnatural ones. In the same way the men also abandoned natural relations with women and were inflamed with lust for one another" (Rom. 1:26, 27).

"Do not be deceived: Neither the sexually immoral nor idolaters nor adulterers nor male prostitutes nor homosexual offenders, nor thieves nor the greedy nor drunkards nor slanderers nor swindlers will inherit the kingdom of God" (1 Cor. 6:9, 10).

"That is what some of you were," Paul added. "But you were washed, you were sanctified, you were justified in the name of the Lord Jesus Christ and by the Spirit of our God" (v. 11).

A Visit to Sodom

One of the most familiar passages about homosexuality is in Genesis 19. The Lord and two angels, appearing as men, came to the city of Sodom at evening. Lot graciously invited them to spend the night in his home. But before they went to sleep, the men of the city surrounded the house. "Where are the men who came to you tonight?" they demanded. "Bring them out to us so that we can have sex with them" (v. 5).

Such flagrant wickedness is the reason the Lord destroyed the city (vv. 12, 13). Yet some today claim that this story has no relevance to the modern issue of homosexuality. The sin of Sodom was inhospitality, they say, or pride or disregard for the poor.

The people of Sodom were clearly inhospitable. They were proud, wealthy, and had no concern for the poor (Ezek.

16:49). But they also committed sexual abominations. It was this sin that caused their destruction.

A brochure from a pro-homosexual church asks, "Why do all the other passages of Scripture referring to this account [Sodom] fail to raise the issue of homosexuality?" That question ignores the words of Jude:

"In a similar way, Sodom and Gomorrah and the surrounding towns gave themselves up to sexual immorality and perversion. They serve as an example of those who suffer the punishment of eternal fire" (v. 7).

The message could not be clearer. If the Bible does not teach that sodomy is a sin, it doesn't teach anything is a sin.

Hating Sin, Loving Sinners

How do people respond today when we say that homosexual behavior is a sin? They say we are homophobes, that we are filled with hate.

Someone has said that this accusation is like calling the Surgeon General a smokophobe. When he put the health warning on cigarette packages, did that prove he hated smokers? Most smokers probably have family members who have tried to dissuade them from smoking. Is that because of hate? No! It's because of love.

A study of First John makes it clear that we must not hate. "Anyone who claims to be in the light but hates his brother is still in the darkness" (2:9). "Dear children, let us not love with words or tongue but with actions and in truth" (3:18). "Whoever does not love does not know God, because God is love" (4:8).

The Christian position is that we must love the sinner but hate the sin. I think robbery is a terrible sin, and I hate it. I think rape is a terrible sin, and I hate it. I think the same about murder and many other sins. But that doesn't mean I hate the people who do them. I have counseled with them and prayed for them and witnessed to them.

Likewise, I have counseled with some who have committed homosexual sin. I know some who have come out of that lifestyle. I know some who are still struggling to overcome it. And I know others who want to stay there. As followers of Christ, our prayer must be that all will be set free.

What Does the Bible Say?

The Bible, as God's word, reveals God's moral character and it shapes the moral character of the Christian. There have been those who have used the Bible to support homosexuality, taken verses out of context and reading into them scenarios that are not there. Quite simply, the Bible condemns homosexuality as a sin. Let's look at what it says.

Leviticus 18:22, "You shall not lie with a male as one lies with a female; it is an abomination."

Leviticus 20:13, "If there is a man who lies with a male as those who lie with a woman, both of them have committed a detestable act; they shall surely be put to death. Their blood-guiltness is upon them."

1 Corinthians 6:9–10, "Or do you not know that the unrighteous shall not inherit the kingdom of God? Do not be deceived; neither fornicators, nor idolaters, nor adulterers, nor effeminate, nor homosexuals, nor thieves, nor the covetous, nor drunkards, nor revilers, nor swindlers, shall inherit the kingdom of God."

Romans 1:26–28, "For this reason God gave them over to degrading passions; for their women exchanged the natural function for that which is unnatural, and in the same way also the men abandoned the natural function of the woman and burned in their desire toward one another, men with men committing indecent acts and receiving in their own persons the due penalty of their error. And just as they did not see fit to acknowledge God any longer, God gave them over to a depraved mind, to do those things which are not proper."

Matthew J. Slick, "Christianity and Homosexuality," www.inthelight.org, 2002.

What Are the Facts?

Tragically, some today insist that people can't be set free from homosexuality. They say it is something they are born with, that there is nothing they can do about it.

The Kinsey Report claimed that 10 percent of American men were homosexuals. More reliable studies of recent years have put the total closer to 1 or 2 percent. One study showed that 2 percent of American men admitted some homosexual activity in the past, but not in the present. This suggests that there may be more ex-homosexuals in America than active homosexuals. So much for the lie that people can't change!

What about recent studies indicating that homosexuality may be genetic? Each of those studies has serious scientific flaws. But even if the studies suggest predisposing factors, they do not prove determinative factors. People have different kinds of personalities. Some are aggressive, others shy. Some have tendencies toward alcoholism or hot-headedness. That does not mean society should put its imprimatur on those things as being right.

Redefining Deviancy

Christians in America need to understand the goals of the homosexual activists. Now that homosexuals have gotten themselves into positions of influence, they are trying to move society in their direction.

The process involves two parts: *D.D. Down* and *D.D. Up.* The first means "defining deviancy down." When deviancy becomes prevalent in a society, people tend to make the definition of deviancy smaller. Otherwise, it is too uncomfortable to deal with. An example of this occurred several years ago when the American Psychiatric Society declared that homosexuality was no longer a pathological condition.

D.D. Up is the opposite. It means taking what has always been known as normal and defining that up into deviancy. As one writer explains, "That distracts us from real deviancy and gives us the feeling that, despite the murder and mayhem and madness around us, we are really preserving and policing our norms."

Do you know who the new social deviates are? Anyone who says that homosexuality is wrong or sinful. That's why homosexual rights activists march in front of churches with signs saying, "Stop the Hate." (They don't mention the threats or vandalism committed by some radical homosexuals.)

Churches are not the only target. Today there are psychologists and psychiatrists who seek to restore homosexuals to a heterosexual lifestyle. Attempts are being made to have such therapists declared unethical. They are abusing psychiatry, the activists say.

The homosexual agenda may be most dangerous in the public schools. One study suggests that 26 percent of 12-year-old boys have sexual ambiguities. By age 17, that drops to 5 percent, and by age 21 probably to about 2 percent. But in some schools young children are hearing that "Heather has two mommies" and "Johnny has two daddies"—and that it's perfectly normal. Talk about creating sexual confusion!

Taking Our Stand

When Lot resisted the demands of the men of Sodom, they accused him of being judgmental. "This fellow came here as an alien, and now he wants to play the judge!" (Gen. 19:9). We will probably hear similar accusations.

In addition, homosexual activists will work hard at convincing us that they are the victims in this controversy. The book *After the Ball* explains their strategy: "In any campaign to win over the public, gays must be portrayed as victims in need of protection so that straights will not be inclined to refuse to adopt the role of protector. . . . We must forego the temptation to strut our gay pride publicly to such an extent that we undermine our victim image."

We must not let the ploys and accusations of the homosexual movement keep us from our responsibility to speak the truth in love. America is being conned, and the consequences are serious. May God give us the wisdom to wake up while we have time.

"*Using the Bible's condemnations of homosexuality against contemporary homosexuality is like using its condemnations of usury against contemporary banking.*"

The Bible Does Not Necessarily Condemn Homosexuality

John Corvino

In the following viewpoint John Corvino argues that passages in the Bible condemning homosexuality may be irrelevant in today's society. He contends that the Bible also prohibits usury, lending money at interest, but church leaders have decided that changing economic conditions rendered this prohibition obsolete. Similarly, Corvino maintains, Bible passages that condemn homosexuality should be reinterpreted in a modern context. Corvino teaches philosophy at Wayne State University in Michigan and is the editor of *Same Sex: Debating the Ethics, Science, and Culture of Homosexuality*.

As you read, consider the following questions:
1. Name three sources Corvino cites, other than the Bible, that condemn usury.
2. According to the author, how were homosexuals perceived in Paul's time?
3. As described by Corvino, what is the Bible's position on slavery?

John Corvino, "The Bible Condemned Usurers, Too," *Harvard Gay & Lesbian Review*, Fall 1996. Copyright © 1996 by Gay & Lesbian Review Worldwide. Reproduced by permission.

Gay rights advocates sometimes suggest that, if the Bible condemns homosexuality, so much the worse for the Bible. Yet that position hardly works for everyone. Many people maintain that the Bible is the true word of God, and not all who do are die-hard homophobes. Some are social liberals who feel torn between their political and their religious convictions. Others are gay and lesbian youths who feel forced to choose between being gay and following God. To tell such people "so much the worse for the Bible" seems counterproductive, even cruel.

But what is the alternative? Is it possible to affirm the truth of the Bible yet deny the anti-gay conclusions the Church has drawn from it for centuries? To answer that question, I want to explore another case where the Church has re-interpreted Scripture: usury. For centuries the Church used the Bible to condemn the lending of money for interest—for *any* interest, not just excessive interest. Today it has more money in the bank than many major corporations. And its explanation for this shift—that cultural changes render the Biblical prohibitions inapplicable—works just as well for homosexuality as for interest banking.

Bible Condemnations of Usury

The Bible condemns usury in no uncertain terms. In the Book of Exodus, God says that "if you lend money to my people, to the poor among you . . . you shall not exact interest from them" (Exodus 22:25). Psalm 15 says that those who lend at interest may not abide in the Lord's tent or dwell on his holy hill (1–5). Ezekiel compares usury to adultery, robbery, idolatry, and bribery, and asks whether he who "takes advanced or accrued interest; shall he then live? He shall not. He . . . shall surely die: his blood shall be upon him." (Ezek. 18:10–13; see also Deuteronomy 23:19, Leviticus 25:35–37, Nehemiah 5:7–10, Jeremiah 15:10, Ezek. 22:12, and Luke 6:35.)

The Biblical case against usury does not stand alone. Plato and Aristotle condemned the practice, as did Aristophanes, Cato, Seneca, and Plutarch. So did Saints Anselm, Augustine, Bonaventure, Thomas Aquinas, Jerome, and Ambrose, citing both Scripture and natural law. Numerous Church councils and synods forbade usury: for instance, at the Third

Council of Lateran (1179 CE), Pope Alexander III declared that both the Old and New Testaments condemned it and that violators should be excommunicated. Subsequent popes repeated these sanctions. In 1745, in the encyclical *Vix Pervenit*, Benedict XIV pronounced that "any gain which exceeds the amount the creditor gave is illicit and usurious." Protestant opponents of usury included Martin Luther, Philipp Melanchthon, and Ulrich Zwingli. Nor is this condemnation unique to the Judeo-Christian tradition: the Koran condemns usury as well (2:275, 3:130). In short, the case against usury, like the case against homosexuality, appears to have strong biblical, philosophical, patristic, ecclesiastical, and theological grounds.

So what happened? Did the Church suddenly realize that it was missing out on something lucrative, and rescind its earlier prohibition? Not surprisingly, Church leaders offer quite a different explanation. According to them, economic conditions have changed substantially since biblical times, such that usury no longer has the same consequences as it did when the prohibitions were issued. Thus, the prohibitions no longer apply. As Father Richard McBrien, former chair of the University of Notre Dame theology department, writes,

> The teaching on usury changed because certain theologians in the sixteenth century concluded that economic conditions had changed, making the old condemnations obsolete, and that the experience of lay Christians had to be listened to. Thus, Navarrus (d. 1586), a professor at Salamanca in Spain and author of a *Manual for Confessors*, argued that an "infinite number of decent Christians" were engaged in exchange-banking, and he objected to any analysis which would "damn the whole world."

McBrien's example of Navarrus is helpful here, for it shows how the Church's pastoral experience influenced its understanding of Scripture. Faced with otherwise "decent Christians" engaging in a traditionally forbidden practice, the Church reexamined the earlier prohibitions and found that they depended on conditions that no longer held.

Disproving Stereotypes

Today, are we not in a similar position regarding homosexuality? Even Christian traditionalists have begun to recognize that the stereotype of gays as corrupt, hedonistic, sex-crazed heathens is insupportable. On the contrary, many gay and lesbian relationships appear loving, nurturing, and fulfilling. As Richard B. Hays, a Methodist professor of New Testament at Duke, points out, "There are numerous homosexual Christians whose lives show signs of the presence of God, whose work in ministry is genuine and effective. How is such experiential evidence to be assessed?"

Interpreting the Bible

Fundamentalist and literalist Christians claim to take the Bible as the literal word of God. This position is illogical. The original books of the Bible were primarily written in Hebrew and Greek, and the Bible was subsequently translated into many languages. Anyone studying foreign or ancient languages knows that translation is already an interpretation. Fundamentalists claim that the King James Version of the Bible is the literal word of God. This amounts to saying that an English interpretation of the original biblical texts written in Hebrew, some Aramaic, and Greek is the literal word of God. There is an inherent contradiction in such a statement because it elevates the English interpretation of the original text to the literal word of God. This is not to say that a person cannot encounter the word of God in the Bible, for the Word is larger than the words within the scriptures.

Robert E. Goss, *Queering Christ: Beyond Jesus Acted Up.* Cleveland: Pilgrim, 2002.

Hays is appealing to a familiar Biblical principle here: "By their fruits ye shall know them" (Matthew 7:20). Surprisingly, however, he ultimately concludes that homosexual relationships are immoral. I suggest that Hays, and countless other theologians like him, have dropped the ball. They notice that many gay and lesbian relationships manifest themselves as good, but cannot reconcile this experiential evidence with the scriptural prohibitions that they've been taught. What they fail to notice is that the Church's history on usury provides a way out of this apparent dilemma.

Consider the first chapter of Paul's letter to the Romans, perhaps the most problematic text for gay and lesbian advocates. Paul writes of Gentiles who have given themselves up to "dishonorable passions. Their women exchanged natural relations for unnatural, and the men likewise gave up natural relations with women and were consumed with passion for one another, men committing shameless acts with men and receiving in their own persons due penalty for their error" (1:26–7).

It seems fairly clear that Paul viewed such acts as a sign and consequence of the Fall. (Some, like John Boswell and William Countryman, have argued that Paul's use of "unnatural"—*para physin*—carries no moral force. My argument does not require this conclusion, but if it is true, so much the better.) Granting that Paul morally condemned such relationships, must contemporary Christians condemn homosexual relationships as well? Not necessarily. Suppose that in Paul's time homosexual relationships were typically exploitative, paganistic, or pederastic—which they were, according to most scholars. If Paul condemned homosexuality because it had such features, but such features are no longer typical, then Paul's condemnation no longer applies. Substantial changes in cultural context have altered the meaning and consequences—and thus the moral value—of homosexual relationships.

The Authenticity of Experience

In short, using the Bible's condemnations of homosexuality against contemporary homosexuality is like using its condemnations of usury against contemporary banking. This context-sensitive approach preserves not only the inerrancy of the Bible but also the authenticity of experience. For the religious believer, both are important: surely the Creator of all things reveals himself in lived experience as well as ancient texts.

But does this approach leave any room for mystery or for faith? If we need only consult experiential evidence to determine God's will, of what use is the Bible? I have not suggested that we need *only* consult experiential evidence; I have merely suggested that experiential evidence, like Biblical evidence, is an important source of revelation. Nor have I denied that biblical evidence may contradict experiential evidence and thus result in mystery. In this case, however, the contradiction is merely apparent. There is still room for mysteries of faith; this just happens not to be one of them.

The usury analogy also provides a better model for reinterpretation than do the more commonly cited issues of divorce and slavery. The Biblical case against divorce is at least as strong as that against homosexuality; indeed, Jesus forcefully condemns divorce (Matthew 5:31–32) but never mentions homosexuality. This fact is startling when one considers how many advocates of "traditional Christian values"— Newt Gingrich, Bob Dole, and Phil Gramm, for instance—are divorced. Perhaps they consider divorce a one-time failure as opposed to an inveterate sin (though Jesus, who likened divorce to adultery, apparently disagrees). Or perhaps they accept an argument similar in strategy to the usury argument: divorce during Jesus's time had disastrous social consequences for women that it no longer has; thus, the Biblical condemnations are obsolete. (Fundamentalists might accept the analogy between homosexuality and divorce and then use it against homosexuality, citing both issues as examples of a lax attitude toward God's word.)

The Slavery Issue

Virtually no one wants to uphold the Bible's approval of slavery. Still, the Bible's position appears clear: Leviticus states, "You may acquire slaves from the pagan nations that are around you" (25:44). St. Paul writes, "Slaves, be obedient to those who are your earthly masters, with fear and trembling, in singleness of heart, as to Christ" (Ephesius 6:5). Are such pronouncements (and many more like them) context-specific in a way that renders them inapplicable today?

Many believers think so. They argue that during biblical times slavery was significantly different from its ante-bellum American form; specifically, Biblical masters were much kinder to their slaves. This argument concedes that cultural context is relevant to interpretation, and thus buttresses the case in favor of homosexuality. But it also concedes that under some certain circumstances human beings may own one another—a repugnant conclusion. Some believers try to avoid this conclusion by noting that according to St. Paul, "there is no longer slave or free" (Galatians 3:28). Yet this response also buttresses the pro-gay case, for the same passage says, "there is no longer male and female." Erase that distinction, and homosexuality becomes a non-issue.

Perhaps the slavery example shows that the revisionist approach—or, at least, the assumption that the Bible is inerrant—inevitably leads to absurdity. Perhaps it is time for gay rights advocates to bite the bullet and say, "Look, the Bible is just wrong sometimes." For those unprepared to make that concession, the Church's stance on usury suggests a useful and coherent alternative.

Periodical Bibliography

The following articles have been selected to supplement the diverse views presented in this chapter.

| Mark Anderson | "Hope for Homosexuals," *New American*, September 28, 1998. |

Robert O. Blanchard   "The 'Hate-Slate' Myth," *Reason*, May 1, 1999.

Keith Boykin   "Fairness and Faith," *Advocate*, March 4, 1997.

Marylin George   "Sharing Disease Is Not a Right," *AIDS Awareness News*, May 12, 2000.

Mary Anne Huddleston   "A Gospel Cure for Homophobia," *America*, August 14, 1999.

Michael Kirby   "Riverview: A Modern Morality Tale," *Quadrant*, May 2000.

David Klinghoffer   "Gay Okay: Conservatives Have Become Strangely Tolerant of Homosexual Activity. They Should Not Be Afraid to Defy the Zeitgeist," *National Review*, September 1, 1998.

Robert H. Knight   "It's a Sin," *National Review*, August 15, 2001.

Robert Stacy McCain   "Condemn Sin—and Sinner," *Insight on the News*, August 16, 1999.

Mark Regan   "Ellen Ratner, Families, and Homosexuals," *WorldNetDaily*, March 8, 2002.

Thomas Storck   "Is Opposition to Homosexual Activity 'Irrational'?" *New Oxford Review*, May 1997.

Paul Surlis   "Theological Note," *Commonweal*, September 22, 2000.

Don Thorsen and Wolfhart Pannenberg   "Revelation and Homosexual Experience," *Christianity Today*, November 11, 1996.

Paul Varnell   "A Preface to Morals," *Windy City Times*, April 23, 1998.

CHAPTER 4

Should Society Sanction Gay and Lesbian Families?

Chapter Preface

In 2000 Vermont became the first state to legally sanction homosexual relationships under the term "civil unions." Civil unions offer homosexual couples most of the rights and privileges of marriage, including protections in inheritance, property division, child custody and visitation, state tax benefits, and family leave. However, many activists contend that while the civil union is a significant achievement in the fight for gay rights, it excludes same-sex couples from true marriage. Marriage is a fundamental human right, they argue, and restricting true marriage to heterosexual couples discriminates against gays and lesbians.

According to journalist Andrew Sullivan, "The civil union essentially creates a two-tiered system, with one marriage model clearly superior to the other." In this sense, Sullivan argues, the civil union/marriage system parallels the "separate but equal" policy that governed race relations in the first half of the twentieth century. In 1896, in *Plessy v. Ferguson*, the Supreme Court declared that separate public facilities for blacks and whites were constitutional as long as the facilities were "equal." However, most facilities were not equal, and blacks received inferior public education and were forced to use inadequate transportation and other public services. *Plessy v. Ferguson* was overturned in 1954 by *Brown v. Board of Education*, which decided that segregation was unconstitutional and threw out the "separate but equal" policy.

Supporters of gay rights argue that maintaining separate legal unions for heterosexual couples and homosexual couples upholds the same principle of segregation that *Brown v. Board of Education* declared unconstitutional. Just as the separate facilities open to blacks were inferior to the facilities open to whites, gay rights activists maintain that civil unions do not offer homosexual couples the same privileges that marriage offers heterosexual couples. For example, civil unions are only recognized in Vermont. With the passage of the federal Defense of Marriage Act in 1996, states are not required to recognize homosexual unions established in other states. Thus, a same-sex couple who enters a civil union in Vermont risks losing the legal protections associated with that arrangement if the couple leaves the state.

Gay rights activists also point out that the Supreme Court has declared that the right to marry is among the most fundamental civil rights. In 1967, in *Loving v. Virginia*, the Supreme Court legalized interracial marriages across the United States, asserting that "the freedom to marry has long been recognized as one of the vital personal rights essential to the orderly pursuit of happiness by free men." The landmark case ended all antimiscegenation laws and proclaimed that every citizen had the right to choose his or her own spouse. Gay rights activists argue that the same basic civil right to marry applies to gays and lesbians. According to gay rights supporters, denying same-sex couples legal recognition violates one of their most fundamental civil rights.

Gay rights advocates contend that supporting civil unions but not gay marriage endorses a "separate but equal" policy that perpetuates discrimination against gays and lesbians. Offering same-sex couples a "marriage equivalent" instead of the real thing, according to Sullivan, institutionalizes the social stigma associated with homosexuality. He states: "There are no arguments for civil union that do not apply equally to marriage. To endorse one but not the other, to concede the substance of the matter while withholding the name and form of the relationship, is to engage in an act of pure stigmatization. It risks not only perpetuating public discrimination against a group of citizens but adding to the cultural balkanization that already plagues American public life." Sullivan and others maintain that the civil union is a significant advance in the fight for gay civil rights but contend that equality will only be achieved when same-sex couples have access to true marriage.

The authors in the following chapter debate gay marriage and other issues associated with the question of whether society should recognize gay and lesbian families.

"The exclusion of gay people from marriage has a real and detrimental impact on children, families, and society."

Homosexuals Should Be Allowed to Marry

Evan Wolfson

In the following viewpoint, Evan Wolfson argues that whom one chooses to marry is an important personal choice that should belong to homosexuals as well as heterosexuals. He contends that marriage discrimination against gays and lesbians denies couples the social and financial safety net that marriage provides and leaves children of homosexual families vulnerable because their parents are not legally related. He maintains that homosexuals have won significant rights in recent years, but more effort is necessary to achieve rights equal those enjoyed by heterosexuals. Wolfson is the former Marriage Project director for the Lambda Legal Defense and Education Fund, a national organization dedicated to fighting for the civil rights of lesbian, gay, bisexual, and transgendered people.

As you read, consider the following questions:
1. As described by Wolfson, what was the 1996 Defense of Marriage Act?
2. According to the author, why are civil unions not good enough?
3. How are children harmed by discrimination against gay marriage, in Wolfson's opinion?

Evan Wolfson, "All Together Now," *The Advocate*, September 11, 2001, p. 34.

W e [homosexuals] can win the freedom to marry. Possibly within five years. This bold declaration, which I hope becomes a rallying cry, raises many questions—not the least of which are: Why marriage and why now? Who's "we"? How do we do it? And, five years?

Before I tackle those questions, though, let's savor the possibilities: We can seize the terms of the debate, tell our diverse stories, engage the nongay persuadable public, enlist allies, work the courts and the legislatures in several states, and achieve a legal breakthrough within five years. I'm talking about not just any legal breakthrough but an actual change in the law of at least one state, ending discrimination in civil marriage and permitting same-sex couples to lawfully wed. This won't just be a change in the law either; it will be a change in society. For if we do it right, the struggle to win the freedom to marry will bring much more along the way. It is not just the attainment but the engagement that will move us furthest and fastest.

But first, let me tackle those questions.

Why Marriage and Why Now?

Marriage is many things in our society. It is an important choice that belongs to couples in love. In fact, many people consider their choice of partner the most important choice they ever make. Civil marriage is also a legal gateway to a vast array of protections, responsibilities, and benefits (most of which cannot be replicated in any other way). These include access to health care and medical decision making for your partner and your children; parenting and immigration rights; inheritance, taxation, Social Security, and other government benefits; rules for ending a relationship while protecting both parties; and the simple ability to pool resources to buy or transfer property without adverse tax treatment.

After passing the federal antimarriage law marketed as the "Defense of Marriage Act" [which defined marriage as a legal union between one man and one woman] in 1996, the government cataloged more than 1,049 ways in which married people are accorded special status under law. Add in the state-level protections and the intangible and tangible privileges marriage brings in private life, and that makes more than

1,049 ways in which lesbians and gay couples are ripped off.

Marriage is a known commodity, permitting couples to travel without playing "now you're legally next of kin; now you're legally not." It is a social statement, describing and defining one's relationships and place in society. It is also a personal statement of commitment that receives public support and can help achieve common aspirations for stability and structure in life. It has spiritual significance for many of us and familial significance for nearly all of us.

Finally, marriage is the vocabulary in which nongay people talk of love, family, dedication, self-sacrifice, and stages of life. It is the vocabulary of love, equality, and inclusion. While recognizing that marriage should not be the sole criterion for benefits and support, nor the only family form worthy of respect, the vast majority of lesbians and gay men want the freedom to marry for the same mix of reasons as nongay people.

From Ideas to Reality

In the past several years we have turned an idea virtually no one talked about into a reality waiting to happen. A 1999 NBC News/*Wall Street Journal* poll reported that two thirds of all Americans have come to believe that gay people will win the freedom to marry. And we know that if they believe it will happen, on some level they are learning to live with it—the positive precondition to our achieving it. This extraordinary new receptivity comes only eight years after the Hawaii supreme court first launched this national discussion.

We can call the first chapter of our ongoing freedom to marry movement the "Hawaii/Vermont" chapter. Its successes were enormous. Through court cases in both states we showed that there is no good reason for sex discrimination in civil marriage, just as there was no good reason for race discrimination in civil marriage a generation ago.

We also redefined the national debate over lesbian and gay inclusion, fostering recognition that marriage is central to any discussion about lesbian and gay equality. This was dramatically demonstrated by 2000's vice presidential debate between Dick Cheney and Joe Lieberman, both of whom answered a question about gay love by talking about their evolving (and increasingly supportive) positions on marriage.

The Hawaii/Vermont chapter moved the center of our country to the "all but marriage" position. Whereas before the marriage debate, the nongay majority did not support any kind of partner recognition for same-sex couples, now we see majority support for health benefits, inheritance, and other kinds of recognition of our family relationships. That is a product of talking about our lives in the vocabulary of full equality and a happy consequence of asking nongay people to hear our stories.

Declining Opposition

In June 2000 an Associated Press poll put opposition to our freedom to marry at only 51%; the 2001 Gallup Poll puts it at 52%. A 2001 survey shows college freshmen strongly supporting our freedom to marry as well. My favorite poll, however, came in *New York* magazine early in 2001. It reported that 58% of nongay New Yorkers support civil marriage for gay people, and that 92%(!) of gay people agree.

All of this is occurring, of course, against a backdrop of international advances. It has been over ten years since Denmark became the first country to create "gay marriage" (not marriage itself but a parallel marital status for same-sex couples). In 2001, the Netherlands became the first to dispense with separate and unequal formulas and allow same-sex couples to lawfully wed. Other European nations, and possibly the European Union as a whole, will certainly follow suit in the years to come. Meanwhile, Canada—which already has recognized same-sex couples' legal entitlement to "all but marriage"—is also in the midst of a campaign aimed at securing the freedom to marry.

Finally, the Hawaii/Vermont chapter brought us "gay marriage"—though not yet marriage itself—here at home. With the passage of the civil union law in 2000, Vermont created a parallel nonmarriage marital status for same-sex couples, upon which we can build.

It is worth remembering that we didn't get civil unions by asking for civil unions. We got this separate and unequal status by pressing for the freedom to marry. In Vermont local activists, New England's Gay and Lesbian Advocates and

Defenders, and our allies mounted a campaign of public out-reach, enlisting clergy, speaking at county fairs, and then folding in litigation—groundwork that led to victory through sustained engagement. With these successes as our new starting point, it's time for us to open the next chapter in our movement.

What About Asking for Less?

Civil unions are a tremendous step forward, but they are not good enough. They do not provide equal benefits and they leave couples and those who deal with them exposed to legal uncertainty. What we want is not separate and unequal "gay marriage" but marriage itself, the full range of choice and protections available to our nongay sisters and brothers. We do ourselves no favor when we enter this civil rights discussion bargaining against ourselves.

The attempt not to talk about marriage, to have a discussion without using the m word, increasingly fails. The fierce (and ongoing) right-wing backlash against civil unions in Vermont (and the right wing's use of marriage and civil unions as a club against us in campaigns in other states) shows that we do not gain much ground by calling it something else or running away from the debate. Our opponents are against us no matter what we seek. When we fight merely not to be beaten up in the streets, they are against us. If we were asking for oxygen, they would be against us. Our opponents will redefine everything we seek as "a slippery slope to gay marriage" and attack us with equal ferocity, no matter what.

If we are going to have to face opposition and work to engage the middle no matter what we strive for, why not ask for all we deserve? Remember, it is no coincidence that the two states in which we have the most expansive protections and recognition for gay people are the two in which we framed the discussion in terms of full equality.

Who's "We," and What Is the New Approach?

It is time for a peacetime campaign to win the freedom to marry. We cannot win equality by focusing just on one court case or the next legislative battle—or by lurching from crisis to crisis. Rather, like every other successful civil rights movement, we must see our struggle as long-term and must set affirmative goals, marshal sustained strategies and concerted efforts, and enlist new allies and new resources.

More than ever, then, "we" means key organizations in key battleground states working in partnership; a national resource center doing what is best done centrally; talented and dedicated individuals who bring new resources and new focus to the table; existing and new national groups prioritizing real work on marriage; and most critically, nongay allies.

Marriage's Public Character

One of the most important privileges of marriage is its public character, which allows our intimate relationships to be openly affirmed and supported by others. This public dimension invites us to reflect seriously on the implications of a couple's commitment. A marriage ceremony itself, whether religious or civil, offers an opportunity to ritualize and embody the coming together of two people—and the communities that surround them.

In a culture that idolizes independence, such values need to be nurtured. We are all too familiar with the unrelenting forces of homophobia and heterosexism that seek to undermine and tear apart our loving relationships. If a legally recognized marriage or a commitment ceremony does even the least bit to counteract those forces, we would do well to support such options.

Chris Paige, *Other Side*, May/June 2002.

Clearly we can—and must—motivate nongay allies to become vocal advocates. Fortunately, we have good models for doing so. For instance, we can examine and replicate how the parents of students creating gay-straight alliances—or the parents, funders, and others who have taken action against Boy Scouts discrimination—have defined their relation to our civil rights and created a public responsibility and role for themselves.[1]

Since there is no marriage without engagement, we must

---

1. In 1990, the Boy Scouts fired a scout leader because he was gay. He sued, and in 1999, the Supreme Court ruled that the Boy Scouts had illegally fired him under New Jersey's antidiscrimination law. The ruling was overturned in 2000.

make enhanced efforts to have our allies speak out in a variety of forums—everything from advertorials to interfaith dialogues to TV talk shows such as Oprah and Larry King Live—describing to other nongay Americans why it's important for them to support the freedom to marry for gay and lesbian couples.

Working with Diverse Communities

We also can enlist diverse allies among other constituencies (religious, labor, child welfare, youth, seniors, business, etc.) and seek ways to work together with overlapping communities such as women and people of color. For example, we can find common ground through joint projects to deal with problems we all face with immigration discrimination or access to health care.

Imagine, for example, a collaboration between the National Center for Lesbian Rights and La Raza or the Japanese American Citizens League, in which each group agreed to send collective information on immigration concerns to its mailing lists and then cohost a program that included gay concerns, spokespeople, and stories.

The good news here is that nongay people live in the world of marriage, and in many cases they will be more responsive to our call to join this work. As the growing list of signatories on the Marriage Resolution[2] attests, many of them have already. We must give nongay opinion leaders at the national level as well as local clergy or organizations the impetus and framework for engaging the public on our freedom to marry.

How Do We Do It?

Our opponents have announced yet another antigay campaign—an effort to promote a federal constitutional amendment to permanently exclude lesbians and gay men from all family protections, including marriage. Outrageous as this latest assault is, there are lessons we can learn from them:

2. The Marriage Resolution is a petition that states that marriage is a basic human right and personal choice, and the government should not interfere with same-sex couples who wish to marry.

the power of a campaign over time, the importance of framing the terms of the debate, the need to present diverse and compelling stories and allies, the ability to make attainable what at one time seemed radical. The good news here is that their attack offers us an occasion to take our case to the people. We should not shy away.

I envision a sustained effort to win the freedom to many, centering on focused work to attain a legal breakthrough in one or more states, together with sophisticated national work to create a climate of receptivity. The elements of this sustained effort would be

• serious multimethodology, multiyear freedom-to-marry efforts under way in the most promising breakthrough states. The partners in these efforts would strategically mount litigation or legislative measures to end discrimination in civil marriage, but the specific vehicles would take place within the context of our undertaking enhanced public education and outreach work.

• development of a clear and sophisticated understanding of what demographics we need to reach in order to firm up our 30%–35% base and soften up and move the 15%–20% of the public who are movable.

• deployment of resources, trainings, messages, messengers, and vehicles to help nongay and gay partners in different states and constituencies communicate transformative information and enlist additional nongay support.

For example, we need to communicate resonant portrayals that show how the exclusion of gay people from marriage has a real and detrimental impact on children, families, and society; how withholding marriage does injustice and cruel harm to lesbian and gay seniors: how the United States is lagging behind other countries; how separate and unequal treatment is wrong; and why the government should not interfere with same-sex couples who choose to marry and share fully and equally in the rights, responsibilities, and commitment of civil marriage.

Let's relate the stories of seniors and how they are denied the social safety net that comes with marriage. Let's talk about the California schoolteacher who died after 30 wonderful years teaching kids, leaving her partner unable to share her pension or Social Security death benefits—or even remain in the home they shared. Or we can discuss how, if the teacher had survived and sought to move with her partner into an assisted-living facility, they might have found themselves forbidden to live together.

Harming Children

Marriage discrimination wreaks real harms—kids teased because they don't have a "real family," a non-biological parent told he or she cannot pick up an ailing child at the school because of not being legally related, couples unable to transfer income or property between them.

Let's trace the experiences—good and bad—of the 2,000-plus couples that have joined in civil union in Vermont. Let's pick up on reports such as the 1999 Stanford University study that showed how denying marriage to same-sex couples hurts kids. Let's describe the cruel sundering of binational couples, the partners turned away at hospitals, the callous dismissal of a lifetime of love in cases such as Sharon Smith's claim for wrongful death when her partner [Diane Whipple] was killed in a horrible dog mauling in 2001. Let's also convey the strengths and vibrancy of many gay and lesbian couples such as my former clients Richard and Ron, who just celebrated their 31st anniversary, or my friends Jamie and Mark, who gathered friends and family from around the country to celebrate their wedding in a lovely church ceremony. Let's make sure that America hears the voice of Jamie's father, describing his growth in acceptance and wish that society could now do the same. Our job is to develop and deploy a strategic mix of messages that tell the diverse and real stories of our lives and love in a vocabulary of equality that reaches the middle.

Why Five Years?

Obviously no one can promise this breakthrough on any specific timetable, so of course I mean that this is doable within five years, but the victory may happen later . . . or sooner. We had victory within our reach in Hawaii years ago, only to see it blocked there because of our failure to act swiftly and strongly enough. But our opponents know the importance of sticking with the fight, and so must we. We must be prepared to ride the ups and downs. Our leaders and national organizations need to understand the lessons of the previous marriage battles as well as the lessons we should have learned from the battles over the military, federal civil rights legislation, and the Boy Scouts. Among those lessons: We cannot expect to win equality in one short burst of attention or one wartime campaign alone. Rather, we must lay the groundwork and not just try to cherry-pick the easy wins or "flavor of the month" issues.

Another lesson is that it is a mistake to define our cultural engagement and the work of our civil rights movement by what seems currently realistic or attainable in the legislatures (or the courts). For one thing, our ability to predict is often limited. I have seen us win battle after battle in state legislatures, even when our lobbyists and some of our groups said it couldn't be done; likewise, courts sometimes surprise us. More broadly, the larger work we must do (the multi-methodology peacetime campaign) should not be reduced to the bills. We do the groundwork in order to build up ammo and allies for eventual legislative battles, and in order to create the climate of receptivity to prepare and embolden the courts. Our job, of course, is not to make it easy for politicians or judges (even friendly ones) to do what they want; rather, it is to make it easier for politicians to do what we want—to do justice. We should not dumbdown our demand for equality, for possibilities open up not in some linear, tidy way but in spurts of creeping and leaping. Through our work and by aiming high, we make room for luck.

What Do We Want to Build Now?

[The year 2000] marked the end of an extraordinarily successful chapter in the history of our civil rights movement from the attainment of "gay marriage" to the nongay response against the Boy Scouts' discrimination. Now, in this next chapter, each of us must ask what we want to create for the young gay and nongay people watching our work and finding their voice.

To me the answer is clear: Let us build not a building or a halfway house or a better ghetto but rather a movement unafraid to seek what we and all others deserve, unafraid to reach beyond itself to talk with our nongay fellow Americans. Shimmering within our reach is a legal structure of respect, inclusion, equality, and enlarged possibilities, including the freedom to marry. Let us build the new approach, partnership, tools, and entities that can reach the middle and bring it all home.

"Homosexuality . . . is by its very nature incompatible with the norms of traditional monogamous marriage."

Homosexuals Should Not Be Allowed to Marry

Stanley N. Kurtz

According to Stanley N. Kurtz in the following viewpoint, the main reason that marriage is defined as the union between one man and one woman is because the qualities that are specific to each gender complement each other, which leads to social stability. Homosexual relationships lack the complementarity of the sexes, he argues, and therefore are unlikely to conform to the pattern of traditional marriage. Specifically, if gays are allowed to marry, the sexually "open" nature of their relationships would undermine the marriage institution by weakening monogamy, the glue that holds marriages together, in Kurtz's opinion. Kurtz is an anthropologist and a research fellow at the Hoover Institution.

As you read, consider the following questions:
1. Why does William J. Bennett believe that homosexuals would undermine marriage?
2. According to Kurtz, for what two reasons did heterosexual, monogamous marriage arise?
3. In the author's opinion, what domesticates men?

Stanley N. Kurtz, "What Is Wrong with Gay Marriage," *Commentary*, vol. 110, September 2000, p. 35. Copyright © 2000 by the American Jewish Committee. Reproduced by permission of the publisher and the author.

A clear majority of the American public opposes same-sex marriage, a social reform already making headway in a number of states. And yet this opposition, though real, is by and large silent. Just prior to the close vote on "civil unions" [legally recognized unions between gay couples that confer the privileges of marriage] in the Vermont state assembly in April 2000, a number of anguished legislators pleaded for more time. Our society, they said, had only begun to consider the full implications of same-sex marriage; how could they be expected to make so fateful a decision in the absence of informed and substantive discussion? But the vote was taken anyway; the Vermont measure has passed into law; and still the hoped-for discussion has failed to materialize.

So striking is this general silence that one cannot help wondering about the reasons for it. They are not far to seek. In April 2000, just after Reform rabbis had been authorized by their movement to conduct same-sex wedding ceremonies, and as Methodists, Presbyterians, and Episcopalians were debating whether to do likewise, a story appeared in the *New York Times* about three respected and moderately liberal Protestant theologians known to be opposed to such a move who had been invited to air their views on television. All three had declined to appear, and on more or less the same grounds: fear of being publicly smeared as "homophobic.". . .

Although most Americans are indeed opposed to the legalization of same-sex marriage, large numbers of these same Americans do not consider homosexuality itself a sin, and they welcome greater tolerance for homosexuals. Favoring equality, they do not wish to see anyone denied his rights. It is the seeming ambiguity in this position that has been seized upon by activists to stigmatize any opposition to same-sex marriage as evidence of homophobia, or prejudice against homosexuals per se. But a fairer way of putting it would be to say that we have allowed a muddled understanding of democracy to subvert our capacity to speak on behalf of those human forms and traditions upon which democracy itself crucially depends.

Not that the arguments in favor of same-sex marriage are themselves models of clarity. Quite the contrary: they have shifted with the moment, and with their proponents' sense of political expediency.

Perhaps the most articulate of these proponents is the British-born columnist Andrew Sullivan, who just over a decade ago launched his campaign for same-sex marriage in the pages of the *New Republic*, the magazine of which he was then the editor. True to his self-description as a conservative, Sullivan put forward a conservative argument. Marriage, he proclaimed, is an institution worthy of preservation, and society is correct to extend legal advantages to couples who choose to live under its formal sanction. For marriage provides a counterbalance to sexual adventurism, especially male sexual adventurism, and thus serves to encourage the socially beneficial ends of emotional stability, economic security, and a healthy environment in which to rear the next generation. But precisely for that reason, Sullivan concluded, the legal benefits of marriage ought to be extended to gays as well, who if anything stand in even greater need of its ameliorating spirit than do heterosexuals, and who could contribute most to society if brought under the healing embrace of bourgeois respectability.

Would homosexuals actually choose to marry? Sullivan, after all, was speaking of a community—his own community—that has put a premium on sexual promiscuity, as well as on rebellion against everything subsumed under the word "proper." Not to worry, he reassured his readers: while some gay activists and a number of aging radicals might cling to an outdated notion of homosexuals as the quintessential outsiders, in the community as a whole the impulse to rebel was giving way to the impulse to belong. Indeed, his "guess" was that, if only the straight world would accept them, many would happily wed—and they might well prove to be more committed marriage partners than heterosexuals themselves. At the very least, by turning marriage into a shared institution, America could heal the gay/straight rift, make headway against the scourge of AIDS, and ensure that a restless and endangered class of citizens would be happier, more productive, and better cared for.

Sullivan's Challengers

Several years later, Sullivan fleshed out this argument in a book, *Virtually Normal*, which garnered generally enthusiastic reviews. It also attracted at least two vigorous counterresponses: one by columnist James Q. Wilson in *Commentary* ("Against Homosexual Marriage," March 1996) and a shorter piece by commentator William J. Bennett in *Newsweek*. Bennett raised the interesting possibility that Sullivan's "guess" might prove wrong—that legalized marriage would not in fact domesticate gays but rather the reverse: that an often openly and even proudly promiscuous population would fatally undermine an already weakened institution by breaking the bond between marriage and the principle of monogamy. Besides, Bennett asked, once we arbitrarily redefine marriage to take in couples of the same sex, what would be the stopping point? Why not legalize polygamy, even incest?

This last point Sullivan himself was, in turn, quick to disparage as irrational fear-mongering, likening it to the disaster scenarios trotted out decades earlier during the debate over interracial marriage. "To the best of my knowledge," he scoffed in reply to Bennett, "there is no polygamist's rights organization poised to exploit same-sex marriage and return the republic to polygamous abandon."

But at the same time, Sullivan was already beginning subtly to shift ground. In the case of heterosexuals, he complained in his response to Bennett, we have never been in the habit of making "nitpicking assessments of who deserves the right to marry and who does not"; why do so in the case of homosexuals? This was a portent of things to come. From urging that the benefits of marriage be extended to gays as a matter of society's own self-interest—that is, in order to tame an antinomian force by, in effect, co-opting it—Sullivan and others soon began to build a case for gay marriage on the basis of human and civil rights.

Switching Strategies

Gone now was the earnest contention that marriage both solemnized and reinforced a worthy moral code. Gone, too, was any serious effort to show that gays, if allowed to marry, would adopt that code. In "State of the Union," a piece published in the *New Republic* in 2000 in the wake of the Vermont legislature's action, Sullivan conceded in one breath that many gay men had no interest in marriage with its expectations of fidelity, while insisting in the next that even if they did marry, the impact on the institution as a whole, given the tiny percentage of homosexuals in the population, would be negligible. But all that was beside the point, which was one of principle: in a free society, Sullivan declared, we allow anyone to marry who so wishes. And although we naturally hope for the best from all those marriages, the actual outcome is irrelevant; marriage itself is an elementary right, and to deny it to anyone, not only in substance but in name (by adopting such halfway measures as domestic partnerships or civil unions), is a species of discrimination, pure and simple.

Increasingly Bizarre Arrangements

If marriage is loosely redefined, what's to stop even more bizarre arrangements, involving pedophilia (since the age of consent keeps dropping) or bestiality? You could wed your cocker spaniel, legally adopt her puppies and claim child tax benefits for each one. Perhaps large families would be in vogue once more.

Or we could go further and sanction partnerships with inanimate objects. Perhaps Mr. Lonelyheart could register his inflatable doll as his Domestic Partner and claim spousal benefits for it. Others are inordinately fond of their sports cars, big-screen TVs or shoe collections. Why not enter into a Registered Domestic Partnership with your BMW?

Mariette Ulrich, *Report Newsmagazine*, November 18, 2002.

Thus the "debate" so far. To judge by the silence on the other side, the proponents of same-sex marriage would seem to have won hands down, no matter which argument they happen to base themselves on at any given moment. In instructing the state legislature in December 1999 to authorize either same-sex marriage or, as the closest thing to it, civil unions, Vermont's supreme court unabashedly invoked what it called a "recognition of our common humanity" as the ground for its decision. "Our common humanity": who could be so retrograde, or so callous, as to say no to that?

But the fact is that our common humanity has nothing to do with the case. After all, we recognize a common humanity with all sorts of people, some of them even criminals, to whom we would not consider extending many of the normal benefits of society. As a social and legal institution, marriage exists not because it is a universal right but only because, historically, certain human communities have decided that this particular form of personal alliance between a man and a woman both needs and deserves societal encouragement. In fact, a rights-based argument, if it were honest, would reject this social favoritism altogether, calling instead for the abolition of state-sponsored marriage and, perhaps, its replacement by contracts in which personal alliances of any kind would be arranged solely by the parties concerned, in whatever number or gender, and with whatever associated responsibilities, they saw fit to stipulate. . . .

Exploring Marriage

What we are thrown back on, in other words, are the fundamental questions of what marriage is, and what it is for. It was the answers to these questions that gave rise to the determination in the West to give a privileged status to monogamous heterosexual unions in the first place, and even though those millennia-old answers may have been momentarily forgotten, or have fallen into disrepute, they remain as sound and as compelling as ever.

In a great many non-Western cultures, polygamy and polyandry (a marriage of one woman and several men) have long existed; it is even possible that the great majority of human societies throughout history have allowed polygamy even if most did not practice it. By contrast, monogamous heterosexual marriage arose for specific reasons, of which the more venerable has to do with the complementarity of the sexes and the more recent with the fundamental liberal belief in the primacy of the individual. If we begin with the second of these, that is only because it is the less controversial.

Societies that practice polygamy tend to be built around life within groups, where the rights of the individual are subordinated to the honor and fate of the clan or joint family. Marriages in such societies are undertaken not so much to join forever with a distinctive beloved but first and foremost to further alliances between families and clans, and the children of these marriages are raised less by their parents alone than by some larger association of kin. Hillary Clinton's favorite proverb, "It takes a village to raise a child," is meaningful in just these sorts of settings, which may indeed be stable, and which are certainly complex, but where the chief source of authority is not the individual but the group.

That our own society is rather different hardly needs to be demonstrated. In the modern period, families in the West are for the most part based not on large associations of kin with whom we live cheek by jowl but rather on deeply personal ties established over time between two unique individuals. These emotionally intimate ties are the fundamental glue of Western marriage, which is monogamous not only because it represents the free choice of autonomous persons but because anything other than monogamy would fatally undercut the primacy of the individual and force us back either into social chaos or into the straitjacket of large, rule-bound groups. . . .

The Complementarity of the Sexes

What, one may ask, does this have to do with homosexuality? After all, as proponents of same-sex marriage remind us, gay couples can be drawn together by romantic love, and stay together, too. And at least some homosexual couples have children as well—through adoption or artificial insemination, or from previous marriages. Not only that, but nobody bars heterosexual couples who are sterile or childless from getting or staying married. Maybe there is good reason for marriage to be monogamous; does that mean it also has to be exclusively heterosexual?

But that brings us to the complementarity of the sexes, a concept so politically incorrect that even to mention it these days is to invite ridicule. For if it implies anything, the complementarity of the sexes implies that men and women are different—and that, where the formation of families and the rearing of children are concerned, heterosexual parents are and should be preferred to homosexual parents: two ideas that are anathema to radical feminists and gay activists alike. Nevertheless, whether it is a biologically based fact or a cultural artifact, or both, the complementarity of the sexes is real, and it is not about to disappear. And a good thing, too, since the stability of marriage depends on it. . . .

This complementarity is absolutely crucial for married

life. To Andrew Sullivan, it is the institution of marriage itself that "domesticates" men. But he has it wrong, or at best half-right: it is women who domesticate men. This is hardly to say that women themselves are never promiscuous; it is to say, rather, that what characteristically leads a man to abandon the quest for sexual conquest and, as the phrase has it, settle down and raise a family is the companionship and (yes) the possession of a beloved woman. Upon this basic dynamic of sexual coupling, society puts its imprimatur in the form of legalized marriage and, at least until recently, has also put its sanctions in the laws regulating divorce, laws that were typically much harder on men as the "naturally" promiscuous partners than on women. . . .

Queer Theory

In saying all this, I am merely reiterating something that heterosexual men and women have always known. More significantly, it is something that at least one segment of the homosexual community has been similarly frank to affirm: the segment, that is, that acknowledges the difference between heterosexuality and homosexuality. In contrast to moderates and "conservatives" like Andrew Sullivan, who consistently play down that difference in order to promote their vision of gays as monogamists-in-the-making, radical gays have argued—more knowledgeably, more powerfully, and more vocally than any opponent of same-sex marriage would dare to do—that homosexuality, and particularly male homosexuality, is by its very nature incompatible with the norms of traditional monogamous marriage.

Such people are represented most prominently in the trendy academic discipline known as "queer theory." Some of them simply scoff at the idea of same-sex marriage as a contradiction in terms, and will have nothing to do with it. But for others, the prospect of legalizing same-sex marriage is in fact quite attractive—because, in making a mockery of the forms and traditions of monogamous unions, it holds out the promise of eventually undoing the institution altogether.

Take, for instance, Gretchen Stiers, a lesbian theorist and advocate of gay marriage: "Two women or two men who marry subvert the belief that women and men take on separate but complementary roles with marriage and overtly resist the notion that marriage functions to support specifically defined gender roles." Indeed, in her recent book, *From This Day Forward*, the best study to date of gay and lesbian attitudes on these matters, Stiers shows that many homosexuals who disdain the idea of conventional marriage or even "commitment ceremonies" would nonetheless marry for the "bennies"—that is, the legal and financial benefits involved (such as shared health insurance). Far from reinforcing the marriage ideal, then, these couples would in effect be putting into practice the program of cultural "resistance and subversion" that she and other queer theorists favor. . . .

Nor does one have to look only to the radicals for a recognition of the subversive potential of gay marriage. William Eskridge, who like Andrew Sullivan lauds its power to tame and civilize promiscuous gay men, also frankly hopes that the institutionalization of same-sex marriage will in turn encourage a greater experimentation with all family forms. Gay marriages are bound to be more "fluid," in Eskridge's term, not so much because homosexual men will be less constrained by notions of fidelity but because, where children are concerned, sperm donors and others will be incorporated into "novel family configurations." Thanks to the example set by these "configurations," we can look forward to all sorts of beneficial changes in the structure of Western marriage.

From this perspective, in short, gay marriage represents but a critical first step toward the legitimation of multipartner marriages and then, perhaps, the eventual elimination of state-sanctioned marriage as we have known it. Once gay male couples with open sexual relationships or lesbian couples with de-facto families are legally married, the way will be open to even more imaginative combinations. On what grounds, for instance, could the sperm donor and aging rock star David Crosby be denied the right to join in matrimony with both the lesbian rock singer Melissa Etheridge and her lover Julie Cypher, the "mothers" of his child?

The Problem of Polygamy

Enter, now, polygamy, an idea so outrageously offensive to Andrew Sullivan that he held William J. Bennett up to scorn for raising it a few short years ago. But those same years, as it happens, have seen the rise of a movement, known delicately as "polyamory," many of whose proponents are indeed "poised," in Sullivan's derisive words, "to exploit same-sex marriage and return the republic to polygamous abandon.". . .

The most common form of polyamory is "couple-centered," essentially an updated version of that ill-fated experiment of the 70's, the "open marriage." Couples attend sex parties together or meet prospective partners through ads or Internet chat rooms. Some prefer three-way sex, while others have sex only with other couples; some insist on the presence of their "spouse," while others permit one partner to go off on his or her own, on condition that no emotional involvement will ensue. (Of course, exactly as in open marriage, these outside relationships frequently lead, inside, to jealousy and breakup.) Although polyamorist couples are predominantly heterosexual, homosexuals are involved as well. . . .

Needless to say, the loss of autonomy and the high potential for conflict in all of these arrangements do not exactly make for stability, and (as in 60's-style communes) one can well imagine that the fate of the children involved is particularly harsh. But that hardly deters the enthusiasts, who, spurred by the success of the gay-marriage movement, see legalized polyamory as the wave of the future. One such enthusiast, a de-facto polyamorist though she may never have heard the word, is the respected mainstream feminist Barbara Ehrenreich, who has forecast the rise of a whole variety of personal arrangements entered into voluntarily by consenting parties and protected by law. Although entry into and exit from these associations would be free, the marriage contract as we know it would be replaced by a parenting contract in which the parties agreed to provide in perpetuity for whatever offspring might emerge from their shifting liaisons; as for the children themselves, they could be raised in, for example, mixed-sex communes whose residents were both gay and straight.

Ehrenreich and the polyamorists are hardly unaware of the liabilities attendant upon their utopian schemes. Polyamory websites are filled with chatter about techniques for overcoming the effects of sexual jealousy, as, again and again, the seething passion for open-ended emotional exploration yields agonies of personal humiliation and betrayal, not to mention the smash-up of innocent children's lives (which does in fact usually go unmentioned). But, bringing us full circle, the polyamorists also insist there must be a cure for this debility: if other cultures can do it, we can, too. After all, they point out helpfully, many Pacific Island societies have permitted multiple and shifting sexual unions, and the majority of non-Western cultures also feature complex networks of aunts, uncles, and other kin to nurture the children. Why not us?

Why not, indeed? For sheer amusement, it would almost be worth it to see how long a fiercely willful feminist like Barbara Ehrenreich would last in a real Pacific Island society, with its tightly bound groups of kin, its intricate rules of respect, its complex and often rigid hierarchies, and its constant demands for personal sacrifice. Indeed, it is tempting to laugh at all these laborious re-creations, whether in theory or in practice, of some of the most disastrous social experiments of the last 40 years. But they are even less laughable this time around than they were in the 1960's and 70's. For now, in the form of the movement for legalized gay marriage, the machinery of the state itself has, for the first time, been mobilized to sanction, bless, and protect those very same experiments.

Erasing the Stigma of Homosexuality

Ultimately, it may be that what lies behind the demand for same-sex marriage, whether couched in conservative or in "civil-rights" terms, is a bid to erase entirely the stigma of homosexuality. That bid is utopian; as radical gays . . . acknowledge, the stigma arises from the fundamental separation between homosexuality and reproduction, which is to say from the fundamental fact that the world is, for the overwhelming part, heterosexual. Nevertheless, in pursuit of this utopian end, we are being asked to transform, at unknown cost to ourselves and to future generations, the central institution of our society. And we are being admonished that to reject this demand is to repudiate our "common humanity" with those who are advancing it: that is, to repudiate them as persons.

That is simply not so. There is not the slightest evidence that either the civil status of homosexuals or the increased sympathy and respect they now enjoy in America will in the least suffer from a continued refusal to redefine marriage so as to include homosexual unions. The real danger, rather, lies in the opposite direction—in the emptying-out of every last vestige of meaning from an institution already under siege by the disintegrative sexual and social forces of the last decades. If ever there was a place to draw a line, this is it.

"If the institution of marriage is to be preserved, a campaign to settle the issue democratically at the national level must be mounted."

A Federal Marriage Amendment Is Necessary to Protect Marriage

Robert P. George

According to Robert P. George in the following viewpoint, a federal marriage amendment to the U.S. Constitution must be enacted to preserve marriage as a bond between a man and a woman. He argues that courts are deciding laws—such as the Vermont Supreme Court 2001 decision to enact civil unions, legally recognized same-sex unions that offer the benefits of marriage—that should be voted on by the American public. A federal marriage amendment would prohibit courts from legally sanctioning gay relationships without the public's approval. George is a contributor to the *National Review*.

As you read, consider the following questions:

1. According to George, what two principles are at the core of traditional marriage?
2. As stated by the author, what does the "Full Faith and Credit Clause" in the Constitution stipulate?
3. What does the term "incidents of marriage" refer to, according to the author?

Robert P. George, "The 28th Amendment: It Is Time to Protect Marriage, and Democracy, in America," *National Review*, vol. 53, July 23, 2001. Copyright © 2001 by National Review, Inc., 215 Lexington Ave., New York, NY 10016. Reproduced by permission.

Marriage is so central to the well-being of children—and society as a whole—that it was, until recently, difficult to imagine that it might be necessary to mount a national political campaign to protect the institution from radical redefinition. Yet today it can scarcely be denied that such a campaign is needed.

Everybody knows that marriage is in trouble. The rise of divorce, illegitimacy, and cohabitation have all taken a toll. If the institution of marriage in our society is to be restored to good health, a reversal of trends and tendencies in all of these areas is required. Still, there is something unique in the threat posed by the movement for "same-sex marriage."

Committing to Monogamy and Fidelity

At the core of the traditional understanding of marriage in our society is a principled commitment to monogamy and fidelity. Marriage, as embodied in our customs, laws, and public policies, is intelligible and defensible as a one-flesh union whose character and value give a man and a woman moral reasons (going beyond mere subjective preferences or sentimental motivations) to pledge sexual exclusivity, fidelity, and permanence of commitment. Yet any argument for revising our law to treat homosexual relations as marital will implicitly do what clearheaded and honest proponents of "same-sex marriage" explicitly acknowledge: It will deny that there are such moral reasons. Any such argument would have to treat marriage as a purely private matter designed solely to satisfy the desires of the "married" parties. If that is the case, there is no principled reason marriage need imply exclusivity, fidelity, permanence, or even a limit of two people.

Thoughtful people on both sides of the debate recognize this. It is evident, then, that legal recognition of same-sex marriages, far from making marriage more widely available (as well-intentioned but misguided conservative advocates of same-sex marriage say they want to do), would in effect abolish the institution, by collapsing the moral principles at its foundation.

So while it is true, as [conservative commentator] Bill Bennett among others has acknowledged, that marriage in the past 35 years or so has been damaged more severely by heterosexual immorality and irresponsibility than by homosexual activism, it is also true that same-sex marriage, were it to be instituted, would strike a blow against the institution more fundamental and definitive even than the disastrous policy of "no-fault" divorce.

It is noteworthy that proponents of same-sex marriage have sought to change public policy through judicial decree. Where they have won, they have won through the courts. Where the issue has been settled in the court of public opinion, they have lost. The lesson is clear: If the institution of marriage is to be preserved, a campaign to settle the issue democratically at the national level must be mounted—and quickly.

A Time-Honored Institution

At the time the U.S. Constitution was adopted, it was taken for granted that marriage is the union of a man and a woman ordered to the rearing of children in circumstances conducive to moral uprightness. Its legal incidents and civil effects were part of the common law and regulated by the states. There was no need at the time for marriage to be expressly defined or protected by federal law or the Constitution. Consequently, the word "marriage" does not appear in the Constitution (nor, for that matter, does the word "family"). Our forefathers shared the consensus of humanity, which viewed marriage as a union between sexually complementary persons—that is, persons of opposite sexes. The common law that we inherited from England was clear about marriage as the union of man and woman: "Marriage . . . includes the reciprocal duties of husband and wife."

Only in the last decade has our country's time-honored recognition that marriage is, in its very essence, the union of male and female come under attack in the courts. In the earliest phase of this campaign, activists tried to establish a right of marriage for same-sex partners through lawsuits in state courts premised on state constitutional guarantees. The strategy was to get some state supreme court to recognize same-sex marriage. Other states would then be compelled to recognize these "marriages," because of the constitutional requirement that states extend "Full Faith and Credit" to one another's "public Acts, Records, and judicial Proceedings."

The supreme court of Hawaii, purporting to interpret the state constitution, went so far as to hold in 1993 that the state's marriage law "discriminated on the basis of sex." A lower court acting on its instructions then found the marriage law unconstitutional—but stayed its order pending appeal. In the end, though, the courts did not get the final say. In 1998, the people of Hawaii, by a very substantial majority (69 to 31 percent), enacted a state constitutional amendment affirming the heterosexual character of marriage. Hawaii's same-sex marriage case had to be dismissed.

Undaunted, attorneys for homosexual activist groups continued to press the issue in other venues. In Alaska, a trial judge read that state's constitution to include a fundamental right to "choose a life partner." Again, the voters responded by backing a constitutional amendment defining marriage as the union of a man and a woman by 68 to 32 percent. Other states, such as California, passed similar amendments by wide margins without even facing an immediate legal threat.

Civil Unions

Having been stopped by the democratic process in Hawaii and Alaska, homosexual activists decided to press their legal case in a state where it is very difficult for voters to amend the state constitution: Vermont. On December 20, 1999, the Vermont supreme court decided that the Vermont constitution requires the state either to grant marriage licenses to same-sex couples or to give them all of the benefits of marriage. The Vermont legislature chose the latter response to this judicial dictate: It passed, and the governor signed, a "civil unions" law that amounts to same-sex marriage in all but name.

The Vermont law, which took effect on July 1, 2000, contained no residency requirements for entering into a civil union. In the first six months, over 1,500 couples entered into civil unions. Only 338 involved at least one Vermont resident. The vast majority of Vermont civil unions, then, have been entered into by non-Vermont couples. Some of them will surely file suit in their home states to demand legal recognition of their Vermont status.

There is still an obstacle in the activists' path. The U.S. Constitution explicitly gives Congress the authority to make exceptions to the Full Faith and Credit Clause. So in 1996, Congress passed (and then-President Clinton signed, albeit reluctantly and without fanfare) the Defense of Marriage Act. That legislation defines marriage for purposes of federal law as the union of a man and a woman, and says that no state is required to recognize another state's same-sex marriages (though it does not forbid states to create same-sex marriages or recognize out-of-state same-sex marriages or civil unions). Subsequently, 34 states have enacted laws that deny recognition to same-sex marriages granted out of state.

Power to the People

To date, the courts have caused 100 percent of the damage that marriage has suffered as an institution. In Vermont, it was the state Supreme Court that forced the Legislature to approve same-sex unions, and in Hawaii, the courts supported these unions as well. Both the Massachusetts and New Jersey courts currently have cases before them from homosexual activists seeking access to marriage. What is more, only 16.5 percent of civil unions granted in Vermont involved Vermonters! More than 3,200 civil unions have been granted in Vermont to out-of-state couples, and some of these couples already are pressing their home-state courts to legally recognize their same-sex unions, representing a judicial time bomb. With increasing opportunity, there is every indication that the courts, if left unchecked, will remain the most pernicious opponents in this battle to protect marriage. That is the primary reason the Federal Marriage Amendment (FMA) is needed.

Glenn Stanton, *Family News in Focus*, August 1, 2002.

But activists are putting forward a number of theories to persuade judges to declare the Defense of Marriage Act, and the state acts, unconstitutional. They may well succeed. The same year the Defense of Marriage Act was passed, the U.S. Supreme Court handed down *Romer v. Evans*. The case concerned a Colorado constitutional amendment forbidding the state government or localities to pass "gay rights" laws. The Court concluded that the amendment could be explained only on the basis of irrational "animus" toward homosexuals.

The Defense of Marriage Act could surely be characterized the same way by socially liberal federal judges. . . .

At a Crossroads

The momentum of the movement to redefine and, in effect, abolish marriage has brought America to a crossroads. Evan Wolfson, former head of the marriage project at the Lambda Legal Defense and Education Fund, says he will file more lawsuits: "We have it within our reach to marry within five years." The judicial assault on marriage is accelerating and encompassing every dimension of our legal system-state, federal, and international law.

The only sure safeguard against this assault is to use the ultimate democratic tool available to the American people: a constitutional amendment. Pro-marriage activists are inclined to back an amendment that would read: "Marriage in the United States shall consist only of the union of a man and a woman. Neither this constitution or the constitution of any state, nor state or federal law, shall be construed to require that marital status or the legal incidents thereof be conferred upon unmarried couples or groups."

The first sentence simply states that marriage anywhere in the United States consists only of male-female couples. This would prevent any state from introducing same-sex marriage by, for example, recognizing a Dutch same-sex marriage. The name and substance of "marriage" is reserved to husband and wife alone.

The second sentence seeks to prevent the judicial abuse of statutory or constitutional law to force the extension of marriage to include non-marital relationships. The word "construed" indicates that the intention is to preclude a judge or executive-branch official from inferring a requirement of same-sex marriage, or something similar, from a state or federal law.

The expression "legal incidents" is intended to convey the consequences "either usually or naturally and inseparably" dependent upon marriage. The Supreme Court has called "incidents of marriage" those "government benefits (e.g., Social Security benefits), property rights (e.g., tenancy by the entirety, inheritance rights), and other, less tangible benefits (e.g., legitimization of children born out of wedlock)" that follow upon marital status. Another example would be the marital privilege against being forced to testify against one's spouse.

The amendment would not prevent private corporations from treating same-sex couples as married couples for purposes of health-care benefits, nor the extension of hospital visitation privileges to same-sex partners. If a benefit is not made to depend on marriage, it can be applied more generally. What the amendment prevents is the automatic, across-the-board qualification of same-sex partners for whatever marital benefits happen to exist.

Preventing Abuse of Power

The Federal Marriage Amendment has a very narrow purpose. It seeks to prevent one very specific abuse of power by the courts, to make sure that on an issue of this importance, they don't confer a victory, on the Left that it has not won in a fair contest in the forum of democratic deliberation. The amendment is intended to return the debate over the legal status of marriage to the American people—where it belongs. This amendment would have prevented the Vermont supreme court from ordering the legislature to grant the benefits of marriage to same-sex couples, but would not prevent a fair democratic struggle to decide the question of civil unions one way or the other in Vermont or any other state. . . .

If state and federal judges remain free to manufacture marriage law as they please, the prestige of liberal sexual ideology in the law schools and other elite sectors of our society will eventually overwhelm conventional democratic defenses. The only sure means of preserving the institution of marriage for future generations of Americans is a federal constitutional amendment protecting marriage as the union of a man and a woman.

Editor's note: A federal marriage amendment was introduced in Congress in May 2002. At the time of this printing, it had not been decided upon.

"*Same-sex marriage should not be a federal issue.*"

A Federal Marriage Amendment Would Undermine States' Rights

Jonathan Rauch

In the following viewpoint, Jonathan Rauch contends that the states should decide whether to permit same-sex marriage. Most family law is decided by state governments, he argues, primarily, because intimate issues, such as marriage and divorce, are best handled close to home. A federal marriage amendment would strip the states of the power to enact same-sex marriage even if the state's residents voted in favor of it, according to Rauch. Moreover, he maintains, amending the U.S. Constitution to deny gays and lesbians the right to marry would be a disturbing departure from the traditional amendment process, which has always expanded rights, not limited them. Rauch is a senior writer for the *National Journal* and the vice president of the Independent Gay Forum.

As you read, consider the following questions:

1. According to Rauch, what is the only reason to enact a federal marriage amendment?
2. What does Rauch mean when he says that same-sex marriage is a "win-win-win situation"?
3. What is "marriage-lite," as described by the author?

In July 2001, I attended what seemed an unusually disingenuous press conference, even by Washington's standards. The event was the unveiling, by a coalition of church and community groups called the Alliance for Marriage, of a proposed 28th Amendment to the Constitution. The "Federal Marriage Amendment" was soon to be introduced in Congress, the alliance announced. *National Review* (on the cover), a conservative bellwether, had already endorsed it.

What, exactly, would the amendment do? Speaker after speaker affirmed that its only effect would be to stop unelected judges from ramming homosexual marriage down the throats of an unwilling public. The intent was merely to require proponents of homosexual marriage to "go through the democratic process" rather than the courts. This seemed odd, because in full view, on an easel next to the podium, was displayed the text of the amendment, whose operative sentence read: "Marriage in the United States shall consist only of the union of a man and a woman."

Family Law Is Reserved to the States

You didn't have to be James Madison to see that the proposed amendment strips power not from judges but from states. For centuries, since colonial times, family law, including the power to set the terms and conditions of marriage, has been reserved to the states, presumably because this most domestic and intimate sphere is best overseen by institutions that are close to home. The marriage amendment would withdraw from states the power to permit same-sex marriage even if 100% of the voters and legislators of some state wanted to allow it.

One reason to revoke such a core state power might be to prevent a single state from effectively adopting same-sex marriage for the whole country. In 1996, however, Congress and President Clinton foreclosed that possibility by enacting the Defense of Marriage Act, which holds that no state need recognize a same-sex marriage performed or sanctioned in any other state. Meanwhile, three dozen states have legislatively passed pre-emptive bans on same-sex marriage. The country is thus almost 75% of the way to a national ban.

Under those circumstances, there can be only one reason

for a constitutional amendment putting gay marriage out of the reach of not just state judges but of states. The sponsors must be worried that eventually some state's legislators or voters, acting in the old-fashioned democratic way, will decide that same-sex marriage suits their state's temperament or helps solve their state's problems.

Repudiating Federalism

That conservatives would contemplate so striking a repudiation of federalism is a sign of the panic that same-sex marriage inspires on the right. As people usually do when they act in a panic, conservatives are making a mistake. Even if you don't believe, as I do, that same-sex marriage is good because it is just and humane, the attempt to pre-empt federalism is bad policy from a conservative point of view.

For there is a compelling and deeply conservative case for thinking that homosexual marriage, far from being the end of civilization as we know it, would be a win-win-win proposition: good for homosexuals, good for heterosexuals, and good for marriage itself. The reason is one that conservatives have long understood: Love and marriage go together. Marriage transmutes love into commitment. Love is often fleeting and crazy-making. Marriage is lasting and stabilizing. For all the troubles that divorce, fatherlessness and illegitimacy have brought, marriage remains far and away the most durable bond that two caring people can forge.

Though some homosexuals have children, even childless homosexuals—in fact, especially childless homosexuals—need and benefit from the care of, and promise to care for, another, till death do you part. Society stands to benefit when all people, including gay people, have this care and make this commitment.

"Marriage Lite"

Before rushing to ban same-sex marriage, conservatives ought to remember that the real-world alternative is not the status quo or the status quo minus 30 years. Same-sex unions, however viewed by law, are real and increasingly honored by the growing number of Americans who have gay friends and family members. I take my partner, Michael, to the company

Christmas party every year, and my colleagues treat him as my spouse. Because governments, businesses, religions and ordinary people are increasingly supportive of these unions, the likely result of a national ban on same-sex marriage would be the profusion of partnership programs and other versions of "marriage lite"—many of which, majoritarian politics being what it is, will inevitably be opened to heterosexuals as well as homosexuals.

Reasons to Oppose the Federal Marriage Amendment

- *This amendment would invalidate all legal protections for unmarried couples—gay or straight.* By denying unmarried persons all legal protections for any of the "legal incidents" of marriage, the amendment would destroy a wide range of other rights that are important to the lives of unmarried persons. Those legal protections include state and local civil rights laws prohibiting discrimination based on "marital status," state laws protecting unmarried elderly couples who refrain from marrying in order to hold on to their pensions, and even state laws allowing a person, in the absence of a spouse, to oppose the autopsy of a close friend because of the deceased person's religious beliefs.

- *Amending the Constitution is an extreme act.* The first sentence of the proposed constitutional amendment would bar all same-sex marriages. However, gay and lesbian couples cannot now marry anywhere in the United States. Moreover, Congress already enacted the Defense of Marriage Act in 1996, which was an earlier response to the fear of same-sex marriages that have never been recognized.

- *The Federal Marriage Amendment would reverse the constitutional tradition of protecting, not harming, individual freedoms.* None of the current constitutional amendments restricts individual freedoms. In fact, the amendments to the Constitution have been the source of most of the Constitution's protections for individual liberty rights. The proposed amendment, by contrast, would deny all protection for the most personal decisions made by millions of families.

American Civil Liberties Union, "Oppose Writing Intolerance into the U.S. Constitution," October 2002.

Some left-wing gay activists favor the establishment of diverse alternatives to marriage as a way to weaken the real thing, which they regard as rigid and oppressive. It is odd for conservatives to try to help them. Marriage, like voting and property ownership and other encompassing civic institutions, is strongest when it is universal and unique, without carve-outs or special cases. It works best when society and law send a clear message that marriage is for everyone—gay and straight alike—and that the only way to secure the benefits and recognition of marriage is to get married.

The retort, of course, is that unyoking marriage from its traditional male-female definition will destroy or severely weaken it. But this is an empirical proposition, and there is reason to doubt it. Opponents of same-sex marriage have done a poor job of explaining why the health of heterosexual marriage depends on the exclusion of a small number of homosexuals. Moreover, predictions that homosexual integration would wreck civic communities and public institutions have a perfect record: They are always wrong. When same-sex couples started holding hands on the street and buying houses in the suburbs, neighborhoods did not turn into Sodoms and otherwise solid families did not collapse. The British military, after protesting for years that morale would be ruined by open homosexuals, has instead found their admission to be a nonevent. Integration of open homosexuals into workplaces has not replaced pinstripe suits with stud collars or ruined the collegial spirit in offices across the country.

Homosexuality Is Here to Stay

Like it or not, homosexuality exists and is not going away. The question is how to ensure that it is pro-social rather than antisocial. I believe that marriage, the greatest civilizing institution ever devised, is the answer. I could be wrong; but the broader point, in any case, is that same-sex marriage bears potential benefits as well as risks. The way to find out is to try, which is what federalism is for.

Thanks to America's federalist structure and the existence of the Defense of Marriage Act, the United States is uniquely positioned among all the world's countries to get same-sex marriage right, by neither banning it pre-emptively nor imposing it nationally. Instead, same-sex marriage could be tried in a few places where people feel comfortable with it and believe it would work. Letting states go their separate ways, moreover, is the way to avert culture wars, as the misguided nationalization of abortion law so unpleasantly and frequently reminds us.

Same-sex marriage should not be a federal issue. Conservatives, of all people, should not be attempting to make it one. They have been trumpeting the virtues of federalism for years. Here is a particularly compelling opportunity to heed their own wisdom.

Editor's note: The Federal Marriage Amendment was introduced in Congress in May 2002. At the time of this printing, it had not been decided upon.

VIEWPOINT

5

"Children who are born to or adopted by one member of a same-sex couple deserve the security of two legally recognized parents."

Homosexuals Should Have Greater Parental Rights

E.J. Graff

According to E.J. Graff in the following viewpoint, homosexual parents need more legal protection in family courts. She argues that courts often arbitrarily favor a heterosexual parent over a homosexual parent in custody battles. Graff contends that such inequality in the law is unjustified because gay and lesbian couples raise children that are as well-adjusted as the children of heterosexuals. Graff is a contributing editor at the *American Prospect* and the author of *What Is Marriage For? The Strange Social History of Our Most Intimate Institution.*

As you read, consider the following questions:
1. According to the author, in what measures of emotional and social development do the children of homosexual parents do as well as those of heterosexual parents?
2. In the author's opinion, why is it better for the biological mother in a lesbian-parented family to be the breadwinner?
3. What examples does Graff give that suggest that family policies for homosexual families are improving?

E.J. Graff, "The Other Marriage War: There's One Group That Is Pursuing Legal Union—and Its Kids Need the Stability," *The American Prospect*, vol. 13, April 8, 2002, pp. 50–54. Copyright © 2002 by The American Prospect, Inc. Reproduced by permission.

I magine waking up one morning to the news that because of a recent court decision, you may no longer be your child's legal parent. Forget all those times you've read *Goodnight Moon*, those long nights you spent in a steam-filled bathroom trying to keep your sick child breathing. In the eyes of the law, you may suddenly be just a kind stranger. No emergency room, insurance plan, schoolteacher, tax man, or judge will count you as essential to your child.

Sound like one of Kafka's nightmares? It's what happened to thousands of California parents in October 2001, when a San Diego court struck down the procedure by which, for 15 years, lesbian co-mothers—parents who helped to imagine, create, feed, clothe, and raise a child, but who didn't give birth—had legally adopted their children. Many California lawyers' phones rang nonstop until the decision was erased from the books while it went up on appeal.

Another World

Welcome to the world of lesbian and gay parents, where you can be a parent one day and not the next; in one state but not another; when you're straight but not when you're gay. At any moment, your heterosexual ex might find a judge willing to yank the kids after you come out. Or you might hear your parental fitness debated by strangers—on radio, on TV, and in newspapers—using language that makes your children wake up at night from dreams that the government has taken you away.

Yes, the climate for lesbian and gay parents has improved dramatically in the past 20 years. There can't be an American left who hasn't heard about Heather and her two mommies. And though the children's book by that name kicked off an antigay uproar in the early 1990s, by the end of the decade the mainstream media were covering [rock singer] Melissa Etheridge and her lover Julie Cypher's two babies without a blink (except, perhaps, at the unfortunate David Crosby connection as the sperm donor). The lesbian baby boom began in Boston and San Francisco in the mid-1980s. In both cities, after mainstream doctors refused to offer donor insemination (DI) services to unmarried women, lesbians started their own sperm banks and DI clinics. Since then, two-mom families have popped up everywhere from Maine to Utah, from Alaska to Florida. In smaller numbers, gay dads have followed, taking in foster children, hiring surrogates, or adopting (as individuals, if necessary) whenever they could find birth moms, local authorities, or judges who'd help. And that's only the latest incarnation of gay and lesbian parenting. Lesbians and gay men have long become parents the conventional way: through heterosexual marriage.

But law is lagging badly behind this social transformation. Although many readers may know two-mom or two-dad families, they probably do not know about the daily legal insecurity, the extra level of anxiety and effort, and the occasional shocking injustices those families face. Society is still profoundly ambivalent about lesbians and gay men—and about the unfamiliar, sometimes queasy-making idea of queers raising kids. As a result, unpredictable legal decisions about lesbian and gay parents too often leave their children in limbo.

The Kids Are All Right

Is there any reason to worry about how these kids are raised? No. More than 20 studies have been done on about 300 children of lesbians and gay men. Some compare children of divorced lesbian moms or gay dads with children of divorced heterosexual moms or dads; others compare two-mom families with mom-and-pop families that used the same DI clinic. The results are quite clear: Children of lesbian or gay parents turn out just fine on every conceivable measure of emotional and social development: attachment, self-esteem, moral judgment, behavior, intelligence, likability, popularity, gender identity, family warmth, and all sorts of obscure psychological concepts. Whatever the scale, children with lesbian or gay parents and children with heterosexual parents turn out equally well—and grow up to be heterosexual in the same overwhelming proportions.

Not surprisingly, antigay pundits challenge this conclusion. Brigham Young University law professor Lynn Wardle and his followers argue that the population samples in these studies have been exceedingly small, haven't been "randomly" chosen, and don't accurately represent lesbian and gay parents as a whole. All these charges are accurate, as far as they go. But the conclusion drawn by Wardle and company—that the results are therefore meaningless—is not. Here's the problem: No one can ever get a "random" sample of lesbians or gay men, much less of lesbian or gay parents, so long as there's any stigma to being gay—and any realistic fear that the children might be taken away. For the most part, researchers have had to make do with samples of lesbian or gay parents who will consent to being studied and match them with groups of heterosexual parents. Does that limitation invalidate these studies? Maybe it would if results varied dramatically, but because they are remarkably consistent, the vast majority of social scientists and physicians accept them. Social science deals with people, not elements on the periodic table. Like doctors, they must always make informed decisions based on the best and latest evidence.

Scientific Evidence

There is no evidence to suggest or support that parents with a gay, lesbian, or bisexual orientation are per se different from or deficient in parenting skills, child-centered concerns and parent-child attachments, when compared to parents with a heterosexual orientation. It has long been established that a homosexual orientation is not related to psychopathology, and there is no basis on which to assume that a parental homosexual orientation will increase likelihood of or induce a homosexual orientation in the child.

American Academy of Child and Adolescent Psychiatry, "Gay, Lesbian, and Bisexual Parents," June 1999.

That's why organizations such as the American Psychological Association, the National Association of Social Workers, the American Academy of Child and Adolescent Psychiatry, and the American Counseling Association have released statements in support of lesbian and gay parents. In February 2002, for instance, the American Academy of Pediatrics came out with a report that had been vetted by an unprecedented number of committees and had taken four years to wend its way toward the academy's full approval. Its conclusion: "No data have pointed to any risk to children as a result of growing up in a family with one or more gay parents." Nor, the AAP found, is parents' sexual orientation an important variable in how kids turn out.

So what is? If basics like food, shelter, clothing, and health care are covered, what matters to kids is the happiness and satisfaction of the parents. Are the parents happily mated and content with the way household responsibilities are shared? Or are they miserable and sniping at each other, whether together or separated? You can guess which type of household will produce happier and more confident kids. Harmony helps children; conflict and disruption hurt. Despite the yammering of the conservative marriage movement, how households are run matters more than who (read: which sex or sexual orientation) runs them.

There's another right-wing line of challenge to these studies: shouting about statistical blips. Occasionally, intriguing differences do show up between the children of lesbian moms and those of heterosexual moms. Here, conservatives want it both ways: They want to throw out the common findings because of methodological suspicions while making a big deal about one-time results. But in every case, these variations are differences, not deficits. For instance, in one study of kids with divorced moms, the lesbians' daughters were more comfortable than the heterosexual women's daughters in "rough-and-tumble" play, more likely to play with trucks and guns—although the sons were no more likely to play with tea sets or Barbies. More controversially, a British study found that more of the divorced lesbians' children said that they had imagined or tried a same-sex romance; but as adults, they still called themselves straight or gay in the same proportions as the straight moms' kids. Is it good, bad, or neutral that lesbians might raise their children to feel free to try out all sides of themselves in gender and sexuality? Or are these results too small to be generalized? The answers depend on your political point of view. And in a pluralist society, that must be taken as an argument for freedom of choice in child-rearing.

Judge Not

So what do these children need from society? The same thing all children need: clear and enforceable ties to their parents. Child psychologist Anna Freud once wrote that children "can handle almost anything better than instability." Not coincidentally, trying to shore up a family's stability is the goal of much marriage-and-family law.

Except if your parents are gay. Think about that shocking red-and-blue presidential-election map we saw in November 2000. If a map were to be drawn of the legal situation for lesbian and gay parents, it would look kaleidoscopic by comparison, with the colors constantly shifting. The answers to some questions may be predictable by geography. On others, even in the supposedly liberal states, how well you're treated depends on your judge.

For instance, did you think that divorced lesbians or gay men, if reasonably stable, could count on seeing their kids? Think again. Says Kate Kendell, executive director of the National Center for Lesbian Rights, "The good news is that more than half the states have good decisional case law that sexual orientation in and of itself is not a bar to custody." The bad news is that a lot of states don't. In February 2002, Alabama's supreme court decided 9–0 that children are better off with a violent father than with a kind and reliable lesbian mom. As chief justice, Roy Moore . . . wrote the opinion that overruled a lower court that had sent the kids to their mom. Here's an excerpt from his opinion:

> The common law designates homosexuality as an inherent evil, and if a person openly engages in such a practice, that fact alone would render him or her an unfit parent. Homosexual conduct is, and has been, considered abhorrent, immoral, detestable, a crime against nature, and a violation of the laws of nature and of nature's God.

Even when a state's antisodomy laws are not so explicitly invoked, judicial recoil can be obvious. A judge in Mississippi decided that a 19-year-old who left her violent husband and came out as a lesbian can see her infant only once a week, between 8:00 A.M. and 9:00 A.M. on Sundays at the local McDonald's, supervised by the ex.

Confusion About Two-Mom Families

Things are even iffier for two-mom families than for divorced parents who come out. Most judges just don't know what to do with these families. Adoption laws, written by state legislatures in the late nineteenth century, cover two situations: a couple adopting an orphan or a remarried parent who wants legally to link the child to the stepparent. A mother can add a father; a father can add a mother. But can a mother add another mother? Most judges say no, with attitudes ranging from uncertainty to outright antagonism; one Illinois judge, Susan McDunn, went so far as to appoint the Family Research Council as guardian ad litem for the children. Judges in up to half the states have allowed what's called "second-parent adoption," but in only seven states and the District of Columbia is this a statewide policy. Elsewhere, you're playing roulette: In Michigan, for instance, an Ann Arbor judge might grant one, while a Grand Rapids judge might say no. And advocates try not to appeal—because of the risk that the appeals court might flatly rule out second-parent adoptions, as has happened in the Wisconsin and Nebraska supreme courts and in four other states' appellate courts (with those in California and Pennsylvania now on appeal to their top courts).

No biggie, some people think: Just write a will and some health care proxies, appoint a guardian, and you're all set. It's not that simple. The biomom better be the breadwinner, because the co-mom won't be able to list the child on her taxes or health insurance; nor can she pass on her Social Security benefits or pension. If the biomom dies, the biological grandparents can challenge the co-mom's guardianship and legally kidnap the child. And if the moms break up, cross your fingers for that child.

Many—one hopes most—divorcing couples put aside their anger to do what's best for their children. Not everyone does. We all know how hideous people can be when fighting over custody: They play dirty, cheat, lie, even kidnap, always persuading themselves that they're doing it for the kids. When lesbian couples have such no-holds-barred breakups, a spiteful biomom can pull legal rank. If the facts won't let her eviscerate her ex's right to custody or visitation, she may insist that the co-mom was never a parent at all, but just a babysitter, a visitor, a pretender, a stalker. (Because gay men don't give birth, they more often start out on an equal legal footing and can't use this trick.) A biomom and her attorney may exploit a judge's discomfort with homosexuality or cite the state's Defense of Marriage Act to blowtorch any legal link between the co-mom and the child. And if the biomom wins, it leaves tortuous and cruel case law on the state's books that can hurt other lesbian and gay families for decades.

These cases can be heartbreaking. There's the video of the moms' wedding, there's the co-mom's last name as the child's middle name, there's the Olan Mills picture of the three together—and there's the biomom in court saying, "Keep that dyke away from my child." How gratuitously nasty—and legally dangerous—can it get. After getting a legal second-parent adoption in Illinois, one couple moved to Florida to take care of the biomom's dying mother. There the pair broke up. Florida has the dubious distinction of hosting the nation's most draconian ban on adoptions by lesbians and gay men. And so in court, the biomom is now arguing that Florida should refuse to recognize her ex's "foreign" adoption. If this biomom wins, every other two-mom or two-dad family will have to think thrice about visiting Key West or Disney World: What if a Florida emergency room or police station refused to recognize their adoption?

Similar cases are percolating in Nebraska and North Carolina. If these biomoms win, the map of the United States could become a checkerboard of states where two-mom and two-dad families don't dare travel. Can you imagine having your parenthood dissolve when you hit the interstate? You might never leave home again.

"This is a level of damage," says Kendell of the National Center for Lesbian Rights, "that Jerry Falwell and Pat Robertson and Lou Sheldon and all their ilk can only dream of."

Heading in the Right Direction

Coherent laws and public policies are desperately needed to help gay and lesbian parents order their families' lives. Fortunately, history is heading in the right direction. More and more state courts are coming up with guidelines that refuse to let a biomom shut out her ex, or a co-mom skip out on child support, if the pair together planned for and reared their child. The public and the media are sympathetic. Most policy makers are open to persuasion, understanding that even if they wouldn't want to be gay themselves, kids whose parents are gay deserve the most security possible.

Unfortunately, lesbian-gay-bisexual-transgender advocacy organizations can't change the legal landscape alone. Both in the courts and in public opinion, gay folks are too often cast as biased, the mirror image of the radical right. As a result, liberals and progressives—especially heterosexuals—can make an enormous difference in the lives of these families.

"Children who are born to or adopted by one member of a same-sex couple deserve the security of two legally recognized parents," reads the February 2002 report from the American Academy of Pediatrics. Originally written to be an amicus brief for co-moms or co-dads trying to sway a judge into waving the parent-making wand, the AAP report did much more: It gave editorial writers and talk shows across the country an excuse to agree. And aside from *The Washington Times* and press-release attacks from the usual suspects, agree they did, in an astonishing array of news outlets ranging from local radio shows to *USA Today* to *The Columbus Dispatch*.

So what, besides social tolerance, should the forces of good be working for? Policies and laws that tie these kids firmly to their real, daily parents. These children need strong statutes that let co-moms and co-dads adopt—preferably without the intrusive homo study, the thousands of dollars in legal fees, and the reference letters from colleagues and friends that are now required. They need decisive guidelines saying that an adoption in one state is an adoption in every state. And they need marriage rights for their parents. Much of marriage law is designed to help spouses rear families, letting them make a single shelter from their combined incomes, assets, benefits, pensions, habits, strengths, weaknesses, and knowledge. Today, when a heterosexual married couple uses DI, the man is automatically the legal father (as long as he has consented in writing) without having to adopt; if any marriage (or even some lesser system of recognition, like civil unions or registered partnership) were possible, the same could and should be true for lesbians.

By taking up this banner, liberals and progressives can prove that they have a practical commitment to real families and real children. As an Ontario judge wrote in 1995: "When one reflects on the seemingly limitless parade of neglected, abandoned and abused children who appear before our courts in protection cases daily, all of whom have been in the care of heterosexual parents in a 'traditional' family structure, the suggestion that it might not ever be in the best interests of these children to be raised by loving, caring, and committed parents who might happen to be lesbian or gay, is nothing short of ludicrous."

"[Homosexual adoptions] would cause problems for numerous children."

Gay and Lesbian Parenting May Not Be Beneficial

Paul Cameron

In the following viewpoint, Paul Cameron argues that groups recommending that gays and lesbians be allowed to adopt misrepresent studies on the effects of gay and lesbian parenting on children. Cameron charges that such groups care more about identity politics than they do about children. The fact is, he maintains, numerous studies prove that the children of gay and lesbian couples have more emotional problems and perform worse at school than children of heterosexual parents. Cameron is chairman of the Family Research Council Institute, a nonprofit educational and scientific corporation in Colorado Springs, Colorado.

As you read, consider the following questions:
1. As stated by the author, what are the three sets of information on the issue of homosexual adoption?
2. According to Cameron, what was the difference in self-esteem between children of homosexual parents and those of heterosexual parents?
3. What is an example the author gives of how gay-rights activists manipulate data to serve their own ends?

Paul Cameron, "Q: Does Adoption by Gay or Lesbian Couples Put American Children at Risk? Yes: The Conclusions of the American Academy of Pediatrics Are Not to Be Believed," *Insight on the News*, vol. 18, April 22, 2002. Copyright © 2002 by News World Communications, Inc. Reproduced by permission.

O n Feb. 4, 2000, the American Academy of Pediatrics (AAP) recommended "legal and legislative efforts" to allow children "born to or adopted by one member of a gay or lesbian couple" to be adopted by the homosexual partner. Such a law effectively would eliminate the possibility of adoption by other family members following the death of the parent. It also would cause problems for numerous children.

Promoting Identity Politics

The AAP, like many other professional organizations, apparently was too caught up in promoting identity politics to address all the evidence relevant to homosexual adoption. In its report, the organization offered only positive evidence about gays and lesbians as parents. "In fact," the report concluded, "growing up with parents who are lesbian or gay may confer some advantages to children." Really?

There are three sets of information on the issue: clinical reports of psychiatric disturbance of children with homosexual parents, testimonies of children with homosexual parents concerning their situation and studies that have compared the children of homosexuals with the children of nonhomosexuals. The AAP ignored the first two sets and had to cherry-pick the comparative studies to arrive at the claim that "[n]o data have pointed to any risk to children as a result of growing up in a family with one or more gay parents."

A number of clinical reports detail "acting-out behavior," homosexual seduction, elective muteness and the desire for a mother by children with homosexual parents. I am unaware of a single child being disturbed because his mother and father were married.

True Testimony

The AAP also ignored the testimonies of children with homosexual parents—probably the best evidence since these kids had to "live with it" rather than deal with a theory. More than 150 children with homosexual parents have provided, in extensive interviews, detailed evidence of the difficulties they encountered as a result. A study Paul and Kirk Cameron published in 2002 in *Psychological Reports* analyzed the content of 57 life-story narratives by children with ho-

mosexual parents assembled by lesbian researchers Louise
Rafkin (United States) and Lisa Saffron (Britain).

In these narratives, children in 48 of the 52 families (92
percent) mentioned one or more "problems." Of the 213
problems which were scored—including hypersexuality, instability, molestation, domestic violence—children attributed
201 (94 percent) to their homosexual parent(s).

Here are four sample excerpts:

• One 9-year-old girl said: "My biological mother is S.
and my other mother is L. We've lived together for a year.
Before that L. lived across the street . . . . My mom met L.;
L. had just broken up with someone. We moved in together
because it got complicated going back and forth every night.
All of a sudden I felt like I was a different person became my
mom was a lesbian. . . . I get angry because I can't tell anybody about my mom. The kids at school would laugh. . . .
They say awful things about lesbians . . . then they make fun
of me. Having lesbian mothers is nothing to laugh about. . . .
I have told my [mother] that she has made my life difficult."

• A 12-year-old boy in the United Kingdom said: "Mum
. . . has had several girlfriends in my lifetime. . . . I don't go
around saying that I've got two mums. . . . If we are sitting in
a restaurant eating, she'll say, 'I want you to know about all
these sex things.' And she'll go on about everything, just
shouting it out. . . . Sometimes when mum embarrasses me, I
think, 'I wish I had a dad.'. . . Been to every gay pride march.
Last year, while attending, we went up to a field . . . when two
men came up to us. One of them started touching me. I didn't
want to go this year because of that."

• According to a 39-year-old woman: "In my memories,
I'm always looking for my mother and finding her with a
woman doing things I don't understand. . . . Sometimes they
blame me for opening a door that wasn't even locked. . . . [At
about the age of ten], I noticed a door that I hadn't yet
opened. Inside I saw a big bed. My mother sat up suddenly
and stared at me. She was with B. . . . and then B. shouted,
'You f***ing sneaking brat!' My mother never said a word.
[Then came N.] I came to hate N. because of the way she and
my mother fought every night. They screamed and bickered
and whined and pouted over everything. N. closed my

mother's hand in the car door. . . . She and N. hadn't made love in seven years."

• According to a 19-year-old man: "When I was about 7, my mother told me that this woman, D., was going to stay with us for a while—and she never left! I didn't think anything much about it until I was about 10. . . . It just became obvious because she and my mother were sleeping together. A few months after D. left, my mother started to see another woman, but that didn't last. Then she got involved with a different woman . . . ; she'd be violent toward my mother. . . . After that she started to go on marches and to women's groups. . . . There were some women in these groups who objected to men altogether, and I couldn't cope with that.". . .

Selective Research

The AAP ignored every comparative study of children that showed those with homosexual parents experiencing more problems. These include the largest comparative study, reported in 1996 by Sotirios Sarantakos in the journal, *Children Australia*, of 58 elementary school children raised by coupled homosexual parents who were closely matched (by age, sex, grade in school, social class) with 58 children of cohabiting heterosexual parents and 58 raised by married parents. Teachers reported that the married couples' children scored best at math and language but somewhat lower in social studies, experienced the highest level of parental involvement at school as well as at home and had parents with the highest expectations for them. The children of homosexuals scored lowest in math and language and somewhat higher in social studies, were the least popular, experienced the lowest level of parental involvement at school and at home, had parents with the lowest expectations for them and least frequently expressed higher educational and career expectations.

Yet the AAP said that studies have "failed to document any differences between such groups on . . . academic success." The organization's report also ignored the only empirical study based upon a random sample that reported on 17 adults (out of a sample of 5,182) with homosexual parents. Detailed by Cameron and Cameron in the journal *Adolescence* in 1996, the 17 were disproportionately apt to report sexual relations with their parents, more apt to report a less than exclusively heterosexual orientation, more frequently reported gender dissatisfaction and were more apt to report that their first sexual experience was homosexual.

'Mummies, I think I'm straight.'

Heath. © 1994 by Michael Heath. Reprinted with permission.

The AAP report also seemingly ignored a 1998 Psychological Reports study by Cameron and Cameron that included the largest number of children with homosexual parents. That study compared 73 children of homosexuals with 105 children of heterosexuals. Of the 66 problems cited by panels of judges who extensively reviewed the living conditions and psychological reactions of children of homosexuals undergoing a divorce from heterosexuals, 64 (97 percent) were attributed to the homosexual parent.

Misrepresenting Findings

Finally, while ignoring studies that contradicted its own conclusions, the AAP misrepresented numerous findings from the limited literature it cited. Thus, researcher Sharon Huggins compared 18 children of 16 volunteer/lesbian mothers with 18 children of 16 volunteer/heterosexual/divorced mothers on self-esteem. Huggins reported statistically nonsignificant differences between the 19 children of mothers who were not living with a lover versus the 17 children of mothers who were living with a lover; and, further, that [the four] "adolescent daughters with high self-esteem had been told of their mother's lesbianism at a mean age of 6.0 years. In contrast, [the five] adolescent daughters with low self-esteem had been told at a mean age of 9.6 years" and "three of four of the mothers with high self-esteem daughters were currently living with lesbian lovers, but only one of four of the lesbian mothers with low self-esteem daughters was currently living with a lesbian lover."

The AAP cited Huggins as proving that "children's self-esteem has been shown to be higher among adolescents whose mothers (of any sexual orientation) were in a new partnered relationship after divorce, compared with those whose mother remained single, and among those who found out at a younger age that their parent was homosexual, compared with those who found out when they were older," thus transforming statistical nonevents based on niggling numbers of volunteers into important differences—twice in one sentence!

Lower Life Expectancy

We have examined more than 10,000 obituaries of homosexuals: The median age of death for lesbians was in the 40s to 50s; for homosexuals it was in the 40s. Most Americans live into their 70s. Yet in the 1996 U.S. government sex survey the oldest lesbian was 49 years old and the oldest gay 54.

Children with homosexual parents are considerably more apt to lose a parent to death. Indeed, a homosexual couple in their 30s is roughly equivalent to a nonhomosexual couple in their late 40s or 50s. Adoption agencies will seldom permit a couple in their late 40s or 50s adopt a child because of the risk of parental death, and the consequent social and psychological difficulty for the child. The AAP did not address this fact—one with profound implications for any child legally related to a homosexual.

As usual, the media picked up on the AAP report as authoritative, assuming that it represented the consensus of a large and highly educated membership. Not so. As in other professional organizations, the vast majority of members pay their dues, read the journal and never engage in professional politics. As a consequence, a small but active minority of members gains control and uses the organization to promote its agenda. Too often, the result is ideological literature that misrepresents the true state of knowledge.

Gay-rights activists have been particularly adept at manipulating research and reports to their own ends. For years the media reported that all studies revealed that 10 percent of the population was homosexual. In fact, few if any studies ever came to that conclusion. For the next few years we will have to live with the repeated generalization that all studies prove homosexual parents are as good for children as heterosexual parents, and perhaps even better. What little literature exists on the subject proves no such thing. Indeed, translated into the language of accounting, the AAP report could be described as "cooking the books."

Periodical Bibliography

The following articles have been selected to supplement the diverse views presented in this chapter.

John L. Allen — "Real Disregards Ideal," *National Catholic Reporter*, January 5, 2001.

Barbara Amiel — "Same-Sex Marriage Is OK," *Maclean's*, July 10, 2000.

Francis Canavan — "The Dying of the Mind," *Human Life Review*, Spring/Summer 2000.

Randy Dotinga — "Holy Matrimony," *Advocate*, April 14, 1998.

Don Feder — "Symposium: Q: Would Vermont's Civil Union Law Be Good for Other States?" *Insight on the News*, June 19, 2000.

John Gallagher — "Are We Really Asking for Special Rights?" *Advocate*, April 14, 1998.

David Gelernter — "Gay Rights and Wrongs," *Wall Street Journal*, August 13, 1998.

Jeffrey G. Gibson — "Lesbian and Gay Prospective: Adoptive Parents: The Legal Battle," *Human Rights*, Spring 1999.

Stanley N. Kurtz — "The Right Balance," *National Review*, August 1, 2001.

Chris Paige — "Popping the Question? Our Freedom to Marry Can Open Up the Larger Society to a Deeper Freedom for All Its Members," *Other Side*, May/June 2002.

Jonathan Rauch — "The Marrying Kind: Why Social Conservatives Should Support Same-Sex Marriage," *Atlantic Monthly*, May 2002.

Rosemary Radford Ruether — "Diverse Forms of Family Merit Recognition," *National Catholic Reporter*, June 16, 2000.

Andrew Sullivan — "State of the Union—Why 'Civil Union' Isn't Marriage," *New Republic*, May 8, 2000.

Mark Tooley — "Uncle Sam Should Care About Who Gets Married," *Insight on the News*, August 27, 2001.

Mariette Ulrich — "If We Try to Make All 'Marriages' Equal, They Merely Become Equally Meaningless," *Report Newsmagazine*, November 18, 2002.

For Further Discussion

Chapter 1

1. Warren C. Lathe III argues that some scientists have found differences in the brain anatomies between homosexual men and heterosexual men that imply that homosexuality has a biological origin. Paul Cameron maintains that homosexuality results from various social, cultural, and familial influences. Whose evidence do you find most convincing and why?

2. In Sue Bohlin's opinion conversion therapy has helped numerous homosexuals find happiness as heterosexuals. Douglas C. Haldeman maintains that reparative therapies have been ineffective and often cause psychological harm to participants. With whose argument do you most agree? Explain.

3. According to Patricia Nell Warren, people choose whether they live as homosexual, heterosexual, or bisexual, and society should respect their decision. Do you agree with her argument? Why or why not?

4. James Dobson contends that homosexuality is a mental disorder that can be treated. He argues that parents must monitor their children for signs of "pre-homosexuality," which can manifest as preferences for symbols of the opposite sex. Do you agree that preferring the games, toys, and clothes typically associated with the opposite sex signifies the potential for homosexual urges? Why or why not?

5. According to Jeffrey Satinover, homosexuality results from an unrestrained society that has let down too many barriers. By this rationale, one could assume that homosexuality did not exist in times of greater social constraint. Do you agree with this assumption? Citing from the text, explain your answer.

Chapter 2

1. According to John Corvino, society should accept homosexual relationships because they provide gays and lesbians with the same interpersonal connection and fulfillment that heterosexual relationships provide nongays. William Norman Grigg argues that society should reject homosexual relationships because they threaten the traditional family. Do you think that greater acceptance of homosexuality would have a positive or negative effect on society? Citing from both texts, explain your answer.

2. Kevin Jennings argues that teaching acceptance of homosexuality in schools helps students learn to critically examine impor-

tant issues and form their own opinions. Linda P. Harvey maintains that the real purpose of teaching acceptance of homosexuality in schools is to silence all opposition to the issue. Whose argument do you find most convincing and why?

3. In Elizabeth Birch's opinion hate crime legislation should include sexual orientation because the brutality of hate crimes against homosexuals is increasing. Richard Kim argues that educational workshops in schools and police academies that teach tolerance and acceptance of homosexuality would be more effective at preventing hate crimes than more laws. Considering both viewpoints, formulate your own opinion on how best to reduce the number of hate crimes against homosexuals.

4. An anonymous author for the *National Catholic Reporter* contends that hateful speech about homosexuality contributes to violence toward gays. Steven Greenhut argues that people who disapprove of homosexuality are entitled to voice their opinion. Do you think that hostile speech about homosexuals by influential leaders incites some people to commit violent acts against homosexuals? Why or why not?

Chapter 3

1. Tom Ambrose contends that homosexual behavior is immoral because God deemed homosexuality sinful. Paul Varnell maintains that most antigay activists rely on unprovable allegations to support their argument. Do you think that homosexual behavior is moral or immoral? Citing from both texts, explain your answer.

2. According to D. James Kennedy, the Bible specifically condemns homosexuality in the Books of Genesis, Leviticus, and Romans, among others. John Corvino argues that the Bible also condemns usury, a standard modern business practice, and concludes that the Bible's statements regarding homosexuality should be reevaluated in a modern context. Do you agree with Corvino's contention? Should the Bible be taken at face value or reinterpreted to accommodate modern society? Explain.

Chapter 4

1. According to Evan Wolfson, marriage should be expanded to include homosexuals. Stanley N. Kurtz argues that homosexual marriages will lead to social instability because same-sex unions do not enjoy the complementarity of the sexes. Whose argument do you find most convincing and why?

2. Robert P. George maintains that a federal marriage amendment is necessary to protect the definition of marriage as a union between a man and woman. Jonathan Rauch contends that deci-

sions about intimate issues such as marriage should remain within the power of the states alone. Do you think that a constitutional amendment excluding homosexuals from marriage is desirable? Citing from the texts, explain why or why not.

3. In E.J. Graff's opinion, family law that favors heterosexual parents over homosexual parents is unfair because children of gay and lesbian families are as well-adjusted as the children of heterosexual families are. Paul Cameron argues that multiple studies prove that children of gay and lesbian parents perform worse in school and have more emotional problems than children living in traditional families. With whose argument do you most agree? Explain your answer, citing evidence from the texts.

Organizations to Contact

The editors have compiled the following list of organizations concerned with the issues debated in this book. The descriptions are derived from materials provided by the organizations. All have publications or information available for interested readers. The list was compiled on the date of publication of the present volume; the information provided here may change. Be aware that many organizations take several weeks or longer to respond to inquiries, so allow as much time as possible.

American Civil Liberties Union (ACLU)
125 Broad St., 18th Fl., New York, NY 10004
(212) 944-9800 • fax: (212) 869-9065
website: www.aclu.org

The ACLU is the nation's oldest and largest civil liberties organization. Its Lesbian and Gay Rights/AIDS Project, started in 1986, handles litigation, education, and public-policy work on behalf of gays and lesbians. The union supports same-sex marriage. It publishes the monthly newsletter *Civil Liberties Alert*, the handbook *The Rights of Lesbians and Gay Men*, the briefing paper "Lesbian and Gay Rights," and the book *The Rights of Families: The ACLU Guide to the Rights of Today's Family Members*.

Canadian Lesbian and Gay Archives
Box 639, Station A, Toronto, Ontario, M5W 1G2 Canada
(416) 777-2755
website: www.clga.ca

The archives collects and maintains information and materials relating to the gay and lesbian rights movement in Canada and elsewhere. Its collection of records and other materials documenting the stories of lesbians and gay men and their organizations in Canada is available to the public for the purpose of education and research. It also publishes an annual newsletter, *Lesbian and Gay Archivist*.

Coalition for Positive Sexuality (CPS)
PO Box 77212, Washington, DC 20013-7212
(713) 604-1654
website: http://positive.org

CPS is a grassroots direct-action group formed in 1992 by high-school students and activists. It endeavors to counteract the institutionalized misogyny, heterosexism, homophobia, racism, and ageism that students experience at school. It is dedicated to offering teens sex education that is pro-woman, pro-lesbian/gay/bisexual, pro-safe sex, and pro-choice. Numerous pamphlets and publications are available upon request.

Concerned Women for America (CWA)

1015 15th St. NW, Suite 1100, Washington, DC 20005
(202) 488-7000 • fax: (202) 488-0806
website: www.cwfa.org

CWA works to strengthen the traditional family according to Judeo-Christian moral standards. It opposes gay marriage and the granting of additional civil rights protections to gays and lesbians. It publishes numerous brochures and policy papers as well as *Family Voice*, a monthly newsmagazine.

Courage

c/o Church of St. John the Baptist
210 W. 31st St., New York, NY 10001
(212) 268-1010 • fax: (212) 268-7150
e-mail: NYCourage@aol.com • website: http://CourageRC.net

Courage is a network of spiritual support groups for gay and lesbian Catholics who wish to lead celibate lives in accordance with Roman Catholic teachings on homosexuality. It publishes listings of local groups, a newsletter, and an annotated bibliography of books on homosexuality.

Dignity/USA

1500 Massachusetts Ave. NW, Suite 11
Washington, DC 20005-1894
(800) 877-8797 • fax: (202) 429-9808
e-mail: dignity@aol.com • website: www.dignityusa.org

Dignity/USA is a Roman Catholic organization of gays, lesbians, bisexuals, and their families and friends. It believes that homosexuals and bisexuals can lead sexually active lives in a manner consonant with Christ's teachings. Through its national and local chapters, Dignity/USA provides educational materials, AIDS crisis assistance, and spiritual support groups for members. It publishes the monthly *Dignity Journal* and a book, *Theological/Pastoral Resources: A Collection of Articles on Homosexuality from a Catholic Perspective*.

Exodus International

PO Box 77652, Seattle, WA 98177
(206) 784-7799
website: http://exodus.base.org

Exodus International is a referral network offering support to homosexual Christians desiring to become heterosexual. It publishes the monthly newsletter *Update*, lists of local ministries and programs, and bibliographies of books and tapes on homosexuality.

Family Research Council
801 G St. NW, Washington, DC 20001
(202) 393-2100 • fax: (202) 393-2134
website: www.frc.org

The council is a research and educational organization that promotes the traditional family, which the council defines as a group of people bound by marriage, blood, or adoption. The council opposes gay marriage and adoption rights. It publishes numerous reports from a conservative perspective on issues affecting the family, including *Free to Be Family*. Among its publications are the monthly newsletter *Washington Watch* and the bimonthly journal *Family Policy*.

Howard Center for Family, Religion, and Society
934 North Main St., Rockford, IL 61103
(815) 964-5819 • fax: (815) 965-1826
website: http://profam.org

The purpose of the Howard Center is to provide research and understanding that demonstrates and affirms family and religion as the foundation of a virtuous and free society. The Center believes that the natural family is the fundamental unit of society. The primary mission of the Howard Center is to provide a clearinghouse of useful and relevant information to support families and their defenders throughout the world. The Center publishes the monthly journal, *Family in America*, and the *Religion and Society Report*.

Human Rights Campaign (HRC)
919 18th St. NW, Suite 800, Washington, DC 20006
(202) 628-4160 • fax: (202) 347-5323
website: www.hrc.org

The HRC provides information on national political issues affecting lesbian, gay, bisexual, and transgender Americans. It offers resources to educate congressional leaders and the public on critical issues such as ending workplace discrimination, combating hate crimes, fighting HIV/AIDS, protecting gay and lesbian families, and working for better lesbian health. HRC publishes the *HRC Quarterly* and *LAWbriefs*.

Lambda Legal Defense and Education Fund
120 Wall St., Suite 1500, New York, NY 10005
(212) 809-8585 • fax: (212) 809-0055
website: www.lambdalegal.org

Lambda is a public-interest law firm committed to achieving full recognition of the civil rights of lesbians, gay men, and people with HIV/AIDS. The firm addresses a variety of topics, including equal marriage rights, parenting and relationship issues, and domestic-partner benefits. It publishes the quarterly *Lambda Update* as well as numerous pamphlets and position papers.

Love in Action
PO Box 171444, Memphis, TN 38175-3307
(901) 767-6700 • fax: (901) 767-0024
website: www.loveinaction.org

Love in Action is a Christian ministry that believes that homosexuality is a learned behavior and that all homosexual conduct is wrong because it violates God's laws. It provides support to gays and lesbians to help them convert to heterosexuality. It also offers a residential twelve-step recovery program for individuals who have made the commitment to follow Christ and wish to leave their homosexuality behind. Current publications include a monthly newsletter.

National Association for the Research and Therapy of Homosexuality (NARTH)
16633 Ventura Blvd., Suite 1340, Encino, CA 91436-1801
(818) 789-4440 • fax: (805) 373-5084
website: www.narth.com

NARTH is an information and referral network that believes the causes of homosexuality are primarily developmental and that it is usually responsive to psychotherapy. The association supports homosexual men and women who feel that homosexuality is contrary to their value systems and who voluntarily seek treatment. NARTH publishes the *NARTH Bulletin*, the book *Healing Homosexuality: Case Stories of Reparative Therapy*, and numerous conference papers and research articles.

National Center for Lesbian Rights
870 Market St., Suite 570, San Francisco, CA 94102
(415) 392-6257 • fax: (415) 392-8442
e-mail: info@NCLRights.org • website: www.nclrights.org

Founded in 1977, the center is an advocacy organization that provides legal counseling and representation for victims of sexual-orientation discrimination. Primary areas of advice include custody and parenting, employment, housing, the military, and insurance. The center publishes the handbooks *Recognizing Lesbian and Gay Families: Strategies for Obtaining Domestic Partners Benefits* and *Lesbian and Gay Parenting: A Psychological and Legal Perspective* as well as other materials.

Parents, Families, and Friends of Lesbians and Gays (PFLAG)
1726 M St. NW, Suite 400, Washington, DC 20036
(202) 467-8180 • fax: (202) 467-8194
e-mail: info@pflag.org • website: www.pflag.org

PFLAG is a national organization that provides support and educational services for gays, lesbians, bisexuals, and their families and friends. It works to end prejudice and discrimination against homosexual and bisexual persons. It publishes and distributes booklets and papers, including "About Our Children," "Coming Out to My Parents," and "Why Is My Child Gay?"

Reconciling Congregation Program (RCP)
3801 N. Keeler Ave., Chicago, IL 60641
(773) 736-5526 • fax: (773) 736-5475
website: www.rcp.org

RCP is a network of United Methodist churches, ministries, and individuals that welcomes and supports lesbians and gay men and seeks to end homophobia and prejudice in the church and society. Its national headquarters provide resources to help local ministries achieve these goals. Among its publications are the quarterly magazine *Open Hands*, the book *And God Loves Each One*, as well as other pamphlets, studies, and videos.

Sex Information and Education Council of the U.S. (SIECUS)
130 W. 42nd St., Suite 2500, New York, NY 10036-7901
(212) 819-9770 • fax: (212) 819-9776
e-mail: siecus@siecus.org • website: www.siecus.org

SIECUS is an organization of educators, physicians, social workers, and others who support the individual's right to acquire knowledge about sexuality and who encourage responsible sexual behavior. The council promotes comprehensive sex education for all children that includes AIDS education, teaching about homosexuality, and instruction about contraceptives and sexually transmitted diseases. Its publications include fact sheets, annotated bibliographies by topic, the booklet *Talk About Sex*, and the bimonthly *SIECUS Report*.

Bibliography of Books

Barry D. Adam,
Jan Willem Duyvendak,
and Andre Krouwel
The Global Emergence of Gay and Lesbian Politics: National Imprints of a Worldwide Movement. Philadelphia: Temple University Press, 1998.

Kevin Alderson
Beyond Coming Out: Experiences of Positive Gay Identity. Toronto, ON: Insomniac, 2000.

Jean M. Baker
How Homophobia Hurts Children: Nurturing Diversity at Home, at School, and in the Community. Binghampton, NY: Harrington Park, 2002.

Carlos Ball
The Morality of Gay Rights: An Exploration in Political Philosophy. New York: Routledge, 2002.

Robert A. Bernstein
Straight Parents, Gay Children: Inspiring Families to Live Honestly and with Greater Understanding. New York: Thunder's Mouth, 2003.

Wayne R. Besen
Anything But Straight: Unmasking the Scandals and Lies Behind the Ex-Gay Myth. Binghampton, NY: Harrington Park, 2003.

Mark Blasius
Sexual Identities, Queer Politics. Princeton, NJ: Princeton University Press, 2001.

Kevin Bourassa
and Joe Varnell
Just Married: Gay Marriage and the Expansion of Human Rights. Madison: University of Wisconsin Press, 2002.

Robert Alan Brookey
Reinventing the Male Homosexual: The Rhetoric and Power of the Gay Gene. Bloomington: Indiana University Press, 2002.

Paul D. Cain
Leading the Parade: Conversations with America's Most Influential Lesbians and Gay Men. Lanham, MD: Scarecrow, 2002.

Thomas C. Caramagno
Irreconcilable Differences? Intellectual Stalemate in the Gay Rights Debate. New York: Praeger, 2002.

James M. Childs
Faithful Conversation: Christian Perspectives on Homosexuality. Minneapolis: Fortress, 2003.

Peter F. Cohen
Love and Anger: Essays on AIDS Activism, and Politics. Binghampton, NY: Haworth, 1998.

John D'Emilio
The World Turned: Essays on Gay History, Politics, and Culture. Durham, NC: Duke University Press, 2003.

Jane Drucker
Families of Value: Gay and Lesbian Parents and Their Children Speak Out. Cambridge, MA: Perseus Publishing, 1998.

Richard Dyer
The Culture of Queers. New York: Routledge, 2001.

Jakii Edwards, *Like Mother, Like Daughter: The Effects of*
Nancy Kurrack, *Growing Up in a Homosexual Home.* Fairfax, VA:
and Dick Bernal Xulon, 2001.

Stephen M. Engel *The Unfinished Revolution: Social Movement*
Theory and the Gay and Lesbian Movement. New
York: Cambridge University Press, 2001.

Daniel A. Helminiak *What the Bible Really Says About Homosexuality.*
San Francisco: Alamo Square, 2000.

Linda Hollingdale *Creating Civil Union: Opening Hearts and Minds.*
Hinesburg, VT: Common Humanity, 2002.

Noelle Howey *Dress Codes: Of Three Girlhoods—My Mother's,*
My Father's, and Mine. New York: Picador,
2002.

John Francis Hudson *The Lost Commandment: How to Be Gay in the*
and John Paul Hunter *21st Century.* Philadelphia: Xlibris, 2002.

Janet R. Jakobsen *Love the Sin: Sexual Regulation and the Limits of*
and Ann Pellegrini *Religious Tolerance.* New York: New York University Press, 2003.

Stanton L. Jones and *Homosexuality: The Use of Scientific Research in*
Mark A. Yarhouse *the Church's Moral Debate.* Downers Grove, IL:
Intervarsity Press, 2000.

Neil Kaminsky *Affirmative Gay Relationships: Key Steps in Find-*
ing a Life Partner. Binghampton, NY: Harring-
ton Park, 2003.

Kris Kleindienst *This Is What Lesbian Looks Like: Dyke Activists*
Take On the 21st Century. Ann Arbor, MI: Fire-
brand, 1999.

Valerie Lehr *Queer Family Values: Debunking the Myth of the*
Nuclear Family. Philadelphia: Temple University
Press, 1999.

Toni Lester *Gender Nonconformity, Race, and Sexuality:*
Charting the Connections. Madison: University of
Wisconsin Press, 2003.

Eric Marcus *Is It a Choice? Answers to 300 of the Most Fre-*
quently Asked Questions About Gay and Lesbian
People. San Francisco: Harper, 1999.

Eric Marcus *Making Gay History: The Half Century Fight for*
Lesbian and Gay Equal Rights. New York:
HarperPerennial, 2002.

Henry L. Minton *Departing from Deviance: A History of Homosexual*
Rights and Emancipatory Science in America.
Chicago: University of Chicago Press, 2002.

Michael Nava and *Created Equal: Why Gay Rights Matter to*
Robert Dawidoff *America.* New York: St. Martin's, 2002.

Robert E. Owens

Queer Kids: The Challenges and Promise for Gay, Lesbian, and Bisexual Youth. Binghampton, NY: Haworth, 1998.

Jason Rich

Growing Up Gay in America: Informative and Practical Advice for Teen Guys Questioning Their Sexuality and Growing Up Gay. Portland, OR: Franklin Street, 2002.

Ritch C. Savin-Williams

Mom, Dad, I'm Gay: How Families Negotiate Coming Out. Washington, DC: American Psychological Association, 2001.

Alan Sears and Craig Osten

The Homosexual Agenda: Exposing the Principle Threat to Religious Freedom Today. Nashville, TN: Broadman & Holman, 2003.

Edward Stein

The Mismeasure of Desire: The Science, Theory, and Ethics of Sexual Orientation. Oxford, UK: Oxford University Press, 1999.

Julie M. Thompson

Mommy Queerest: Contemporary Rhetorics of Lesbian Maternal Identity. Amherst: University of Massachusetts Press, 2002.

Michael Warner

The Trouble with Normal: Sex, Politics, and the Ethics of Queer Life. New York: Free Press, 1999.

Index